GARDEN RAILWAYS

The Essential Guide to Construction

Chris Hatton

For my mother, for the 'loan' of her garden, and my father, for the ever-raidable box of spares.

3695
LMS

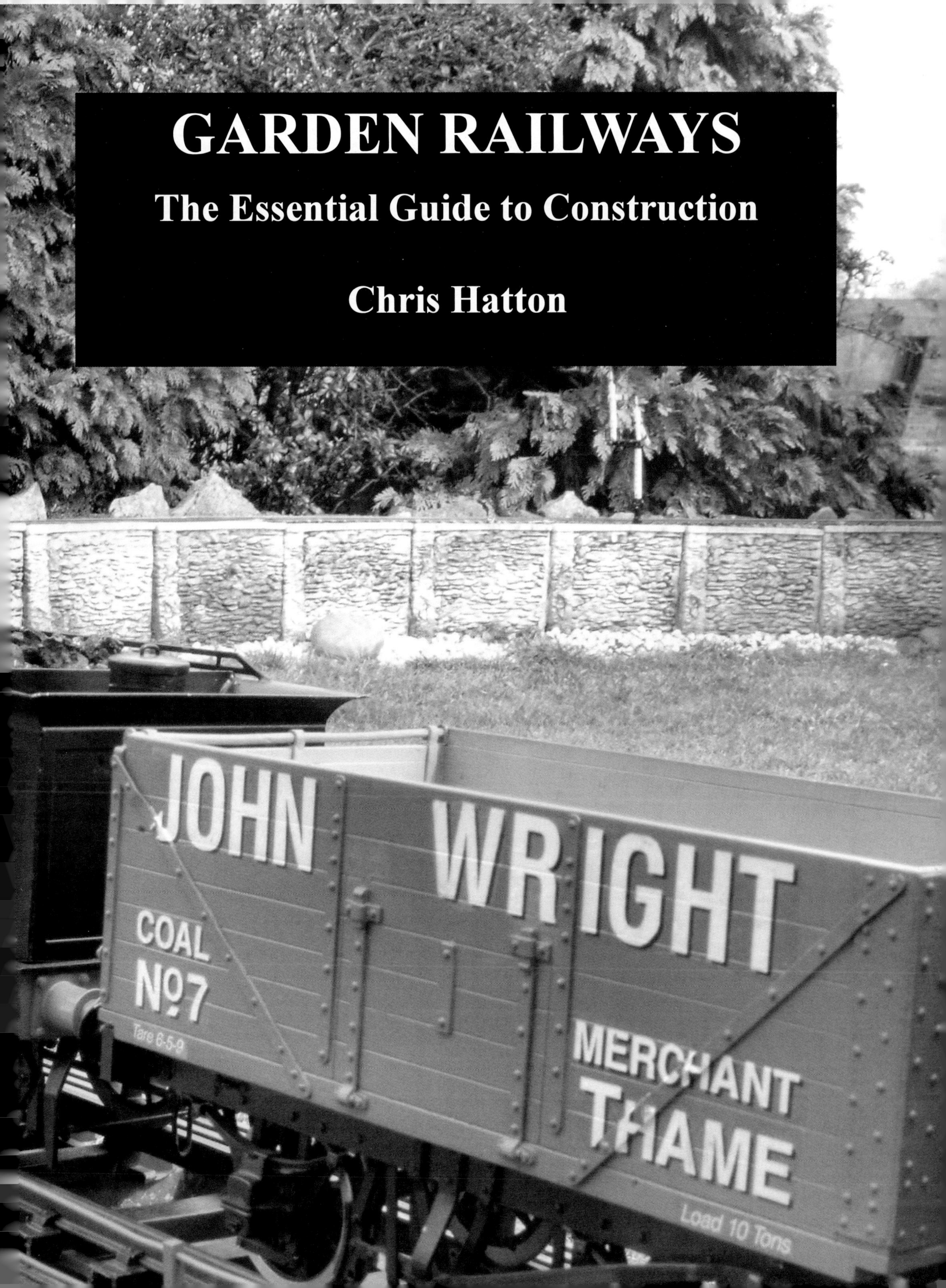
GARDEN RAILWAYS
The Essential Guide to Construction
Chris Hatton
JOHN WRIGHT
COAL
Nº7
Tare 6-5-9
MERCHANT
THAME
Load 10 Tons

ISBN (10) 0 –9554110-4-1
(13) 978-0-9554110-4-5

First published in 2007 by Kevin Robertson
under the **NOODLE BOOKS** imprint
PO Box 279
Corhampton
SOUTHAMPTON
SO32 3ZX

www.kevinrobertsonbooks.co.uk

Printed in England by
Ian Allan Printing Ltd.

Front cover: - A Class 50 leans into the curve on Anthony Delaine Smith's garden railway, a long train of stone wagons in tow. This picture is what mainline garden railways are all about - prototypically long trains, long stretches of track and big engines pelting along at speed.

Tony Wright / British Railway Modelling

Preceding pages: - A freshly repainted Midland 3F heads across one of the viaducts on Michael Adamson's Gauge 1 garden railway. Of particularly worthy note here is the wall in the background supporting the track in a very prototypical and believable manner.

Tony Wright / British Railway Modelling

Health and Safety Note

The author wishes to bring to people's attention the fact that, while Garden Railwaying is one of the most enjoyable and pleasurable escapades I have ever embarked upon, there are inevitably risks to personal safety when using power tools and mains electricity outside. Cement, too, is an aggressive alkali when wet and personal protective clothing should be worn when using it, with every effort made not to get it on the skin.

While I do not believe that any injury should come to anyone intelligently constructing a garden railway using the methods described in this book, neither the author nor Kevin Robertson (Noodle Books) will accept any responsibility if such a mishap does occur.

CONTENTS

	INTRODUCTION	7
Chapter 1	**PLANNING THE LINE**	11
	Test track in the garden or model railway outside?	
	The scale and gauge decision	
	Standard or narrow gauge?	
	Out and back or continuous run?	
	Ground level or raised?	
	Working out what you can fit in the space	
	Planning the construction of the line	
Chapter 2	**THE MATERIALS INVOLVED**	23
	Concrete and its constituent parts	
	Other bulk materials	
	Bricks	
	Timber	
Chapter 3	**CONSTRUCTING THE BASE**	27
	Foundations	
	Concrete	
	Walling	
	Wooden structure supports	
Chapter 4	**THE MAJOR CIVIL ENGINEERING WORK**	35
	Bridges	
	Tunnels	
	Cuttings and Embankments	
Chapter 5	**LAYING THE TRACK**	45
	Building the trackbed and ballasting the formation	
	Common track faults	
	Faults in the line of the track	
	Faults in the level of the track	
Chapter 6	**ELECTRICS**	53
	Electricity Supply	
	Control panels in the garden	
	Bonding up the track	
Chapter 7	**S & T POINT AND SIGNAL OPERATION**	59
	Point motors	
	Signalling	
	Controlling the signals	
	Communication systems	
	Track circuits	
Chapter 8	**CREATING THE BUILT ENVIRONMENT**	73
	Buildings	
	Platforms	
Chapter 9	**THE FINISHING TOUCHES**	79
	Garden lighting	
	Water features in the garden	
	Plants and greenery	
Chapter 10	**STOCK AND OPERATION**	83
	Garden railway stock	
	Operating a garden railway	
Chapter 11	**CONCLUSIONS**	87
	REFERENCES and RECOMMENDED READING	88
	ACKNOWLEDGEMENTS	88

FROM START TO FINISH...

INTRODUCTION

Model railways take on a whole new dimension when constructed in the garden. Constrictions of space, resulting in all manner of compromise indoors, disappear completely - and instead a double track mainline can wend its way between flowerbeds, 12 coach trains passing at speed; freight trains can run to dozens of grubby windcutters clattering up the bank behind a grimy 9F, and an entire narrow gauge system can be built meandering across the garden between stations, branches heading off under paths and round flowerbeds to far flung stations nestling beside the pond. The potential size of a garden railway system far outstrips that in most houses, and an opportunity is provided to build lines which it would be simply impossible to build inside. For anyone who has always enjoyed the sight of long trains running at speed, just as they used to, or who enjoys the operational side of a railway perhaps more than super-detailing a wagon, I would recommend the garden wholeheartedly as somewhere to build a railway.

There always seem to be many more ways to derive satisfaction from a garden railway than from one built indoors. Not only are mammoth operating sessions possible with hours spent strictly following a timetable and sending and receiving trains to and from the other parts of the layout - but the line can also be enjoyed from a distance. Warm summer evenings can be spent sitting on a garden bench with a few good friends and a few bottles of red, watching from afar as a procession of tail-lights disappears into the dusk, signals changing automatically behind one train to usher in the next.

Garden railways also offer huge potential enjoyment during construction, and a whole new range of skills can be learnt. Personally, one of the most satisfying ways I can think of to spend a day is outside in the sun and fresh air, engaged in turning a stack of bricks and a pile of sand into a neat length of walling, laying the track base, ballast and track on top, and then running the first train.

The railway can also be enjoyed in all seasons, unlike a few boards inside which might see the light of day six times a year. It's always out there on display. As you head out for work on an autumn morning you notice the way the sharp frost appears as a covering of snow on the main line, and, pausing, you shiver for a moment as you imagine how cold it would be on the draughty footplate of a Dean goods on the morning pick-up freight. A winter's mist, viewed from a distance while sitting indoors with a modelling book by the fire, lends a whole new aspect to the line - and you pity the poor driver of the up postal straining his eyes for a sight of the distant, wondering with every passing joint if he is going to be checked on the steep gradient with his heavy train of Christmas letters behind him.

You also get a real sense of managing a railway in the garden – almost akin to the feeling you get reading the Rolt book about the early days of the Talyllyn - a feeling of having to keep the thing going, just about together and working, with the weather as your constant enemy trying to do just the opposite. You can walk around the line in a spare few minutes as the windscreen demists in December and notice any branches getting a bit close that need

Right: A single coach battles through the snow in a scene you could only get in the garden. A posed photo, I confess - it was a bit nippy to hang around too long outside, as I remember it – but it does show the challenge of running trains at certain times of the year!

chopping back, or the odd baseboard that has shifted a little since you built it, or a signal which needs a new coat of paint. You can use your experience to judge which need attending to immediately and which you just need to keep an eye on in case the situation gets any worse. Not only that, but the system can be altered and extended far more easily than a model railway built inside, meaning you can always build something new, should you find you enjoy building the line just as much as operating it.

This book is written from my personal experience constructing, operating and maintaining my own garden railway. It centres on constructing and operating railway lines in the smaller scales, up to about gauge one, rather than larger scale narrow gauge railways, as there are many excellent books available on the construction and operation of that kind of line. This book instead focuses on constructing main lines in miniature, a subject I feel has never received the attention it deserves in the books which have been published. Although my railway, around which most of the photos are taken, is 7mm narrow gauge, the constructional techniques and methods described in these pages are equally valid for any scale. Although the width of trackbase on top of a wall will be different for an O gauge or an N gauge system, the construction of the wall itself will be exactly the same.

Railway modelling has always been a diverse hobby and nowhere is this truer than when constructing a railway in the garden. It is necessary to be both something of a builder and of an engineer, as well as conversant with the usual modelling skills demanded by the hobby. I always feel there is a lack of understanding amongst modellers over why some things are done in a particular way - for example, why bridge beams are not built on a curve, or modern facing bricks used underground - and while modellers are excellent at copying what existed in reality, when it comes to designing something for themselves the understanding required to make it look right is lacking. It is for this reason that this book aims

Catching the late summer sun, my Class 37 heads a van train down to Rive Reine. While the bricks and the baseboard could be argued as intrusive, the track 0-16.5 rather than 00 and nothing but the engine and coach remotely to scale, there is something very believable about this picture to my mind. Perhaps it is a combination of the realistic viewpoint and the gentle outside lighting that makes me think, whenever I see the photo, of being at university in Cardiff, standing in the garden of a friend's student house one summer evening waiting for the barbecue to heat up, leaning on the wall at the bottom of the Rhymney Railway embankment as one of these engines drifted back to Cardiff with the return working of the evening commuter train to Rhymney. I can almost hear that 12 cylinder engine burbling away to itself as it drifts effortlessly back down to Canton...

throughout to explain why things are done in a particular manner and never to simply decree. I also find understanding how things will be physically constructed, for example a brick wall, an incredibly useful resource when building something for an 'inside' modelling project. You don't, for example, have to spend hours poring over photos to discover whether or not every other ring of bricks in an English bond wall starts with one header or two - once you have built a few walls, you just know.

The garden also allows for a very different approach to modelling things like buildings and signals to that which is generally required inside. Outside, the overall impression is all-important, and the detail much less so. The natural viewing distance is nearer ten feet than three, and models can be much simpler and quicker to construct, although the overall result can be just as good if not better than inside, benefiting from the increased space available to lay things out on prototypical curves, and suffering from none of the cramped planning you occasionally see on inside layouts.

The actual operation of a garden railway is often completely different from that which could be accomplished on an inside line purely because the layout can be so much bigger. The potential is there in the garden for running a line as a complete system, with no need for fiddle yards to store trains in. The stations at either end can instead be operated in just the same way as the real thing was, with a twelve coach train easing gently into a station, the engine uncoupling and running slowly off onto the turntable just as another drifts out of the shed road and onto the front of the coaches. A short wait for the signals to come off and the train is drawn back out again, accelerating away across the junction and heading off at speed under clear signals, disappearing from view round a

A short branch train drifts up to the outer home at Grogley Junction. The space available in the garden allows a much more prototypical approach to laying out the line, with space between places that you just can't afford to allow inside. Being outside and working with a team of operators all round the garden to keep the trains running quickly and efficiently is definitely one of the more enjoyable ways to spend an afternoon, requiring skill and trust in the other members of the team - and it is an activity so much improved when it was you who built the line and you who can enjoy the satisfaction of seeing it all working.

gentle curve in the distance, down beyond the carriage sidings and the sheds. While all that has been happening a goods train clanks slowly out of the up goods loop and into the yard, the station pilot shunts some coaches into the other platform road and a brakevan is propelled firmly onto the end of a train of milk tanks in the busy dock. I could be talking about an afternoon watching the trains go by on the end of the platform at Birmingham Moor Street or the old Southampton Terminus station, but all this can easily take place within the confines of a garden railway in an area no bigger than a large patio.

With so much space comes the potential for so many more railway features that most people just aren't lucky enough to have room for inside. Not only that, but with space for more than just one station and consequently more than one operator the potential for a proper signalling system is just asking to be fulfilled, the signals heading off down the garden along the main line, each spaced a prototypical distance from the next and controlling the running of the trains in just the way they were designed to on the real thing. It is the garden that offers the perfect opportunity to build the layouts most of us could only dream about building round the house.

I can only suggest you get out there with the tape and have a quick measure up. Just to see what you *could* fit in the space available, of course.

It is amazing how out-of-scale garden plants can be imagined by the mind as trees and painted out of a view, the eye automatically concentrating on the important parts of the railway scene. Here the eye is drawn immediately to the engine shed, grubby clay hoods and the bridge and hardly notices the michaelmas daisies and apple tree that actually form the backdrop to the photo. This, I think, is another clear advantage of garden railways over their inside counterparts. Whereas inside the cans of paint and rusty bike leaning behind the baseboard against the garage wall jar the eye and remind the viewer constantly that he is looking at a model of a railway, in the garden the railway just blends into the scene, and the scene into the railway.

1

PLANNING THE LINE

There are very many ways to build a garden railway; and some decisions to reduce the number of options will have to be taken and some plans will have to be developed before construction can commence. This section aims to look at some of the possible forms a garden railway can take and to examine some of the factors influencing the major decisions during the planning process in a logical order. Personally, I have never entirely believed in planning things in complete detail and then commencing on the construction process. In my experience there is no better way to overcome the design hurdles involved in a construction project than to simply get stuck in – often problems you could have spent hours agonising over on the drawing board simply disappear in real life, or the answer becomes obvious during construction.

There are however some fundamental choices which have to be made in the beginning – the gauge of the line and the basic layout for example, before walls start going up and concrete starts setting. Details such as the precise track layout can be left fluid however - I seem to be constantly changing mine just as the real railway companies seem incapable of leaving their layouts alone - and other details which you didn't even consider during the initial planning can be added later as time, finances and inclination permit. 'Planning something to death' is a very valid expression, and the psychological boost gained from getting your first yard of track down is so great it would be worth doing at an early stage even if it later transpires it is in the wrong place. The P-Way gang can always give it a quick nudge over.

THE VARIOUS OPTIONS

It would be impossible to categorise all the options available to the garden railway builder in terms of different types of line that could be constructed. There are no nice neat lists and flow diagrams which I can produce to explain the various options, as one of the inherent features of garden railways is the sheer variation possible. Is the line to be standard or narrow gauge? A continuous run or an out and back system? A test-track in the garden, or complete with stations, signals and surrounding infrastructure? The following sections discuss both sides of some of the bigger choices necessary. You will find no cut and dried answers here, and probably a lot that you find obvious – but hopefully there will be some approaches to the decisions you have not foreseen and some ideas you have not considered.

TEST TRACK IN THE GARDEN OR MODEL RAILWAY OUTSIDE?

Whether you opt for a simple oval of track on which to stretch your locomotive's legs or you create a

A Barry railway train of six wheelers rounds one of the curves on Dr Bob Buckland's garden railway. This line is a simple circle of track on concrete blocks, the true test track in the garden – yet for all its simplicity it incorporates most of the advantages of garden railways – a continuous run allows the operator to sit back and watch the trains, the trains can be run at a good speed along decent distances of track and the whole construction and operation of the line take place in the great outdoors – surely a much healthier and more enjoyable environment than being confined to the loft.

Photo: Dr Bob Buckland

complete model railway system with stations, sidings, buildings, houses, signals and telegraph poles is one of the first decisions to be taken, and not much of a conscious decision really - generally you will know what you are hoping to achieve, and how much time and effort (and at the end of the day, hours down on your hands and knees) you are prepared to put in.

The two alternatives are poles apart however, and there is a lot of middle ground between them, into which category most garden railways fit - combinations of breeze block simplicity with a line of set-track on top or the detailed re-creation of a railway empire taking years to complete. I like to consider that my own railway, for example, is fairly detailed around the stations and I put in a lot of effort on the easily visible bits to make the layout and buildings appear as natural as possible, and to set the railway in a realistic landscape. The return loops in shed and behind bushes however are there purely to create a continuous run and give plenty of operating potential, and are as functional as they come – walls of concrete blocks or simple wooden supporting structures.

I think the key difference between the two ends of the garden railway continuum is the style in which you intend to operate the line - whether you intend to put a couple of trains on and watch them run, or you hope to be able to send trains to different operators, re-marshalling trains and sending them on to other people, thus deriving your enjoyment from actually running the railway rather than watching the railway run. The sidings, loops and sections will come naturally if the railway is being built to be operated, whereas you will naturally simplify these aspects if you just wish to watch trains go by.

There is a lot to be said for the test track in the garden approach, cutting out the huge amount of effort which goes into building a model railway outside. I have spent many happy afternoons watching trains simply running along a brick wall, the eye hardly ever noticing the complete absence of any scaled surroundings; it instead being the scale length of the trains running at prototypical speeds and on prototypically flat curves that makes for such enjoyable viewing. It is, after all, unlikely that you would be constructing a garden railway in the first place if you were aiming to create a landscape in perfect detail, as such detail is very difficult to create in a weatherproof manner.

There is also the option of a 'hybrid' garden railway, with stations or storage sidings inside and the long runs of track out in the garden, which I hope one day to have the garden for. I have always wanted to build a large railway station in a shed with the junctions at either end of the station, and huge return loops outside to give a good run for the trains and a decent space of time between their departure and re-arrival on the scene. With no horribly un-prototypically sharp curves to fit into the shed and plenty of scope for detailing the station itself I think if I built this line I would construct the outside sections on just brick walls, as I could satisfy any desire for detailed modelling inside.

It is also true that models which start life as a simple line with just track on baseboards can be built up over time to a veritable empire. My own railway started in 1996 and has grown slowly ever since. A few very simple bits of track have been added to by countless boxes of plain line and S & C, and a controller plugging straight into the track has become a few miles of wire with I'd rather not think how many relays and track circuit operated signals.

It doesn't take too much outside to change a few lengths of track into something that looks far more like a model of a railway – or, indeed, the real thing. The addition of a rough platform surface, a barrow crossing across the platform road and an easy to construct station lamp really improves this scene from the simple track on wooden boards which existed here previously.

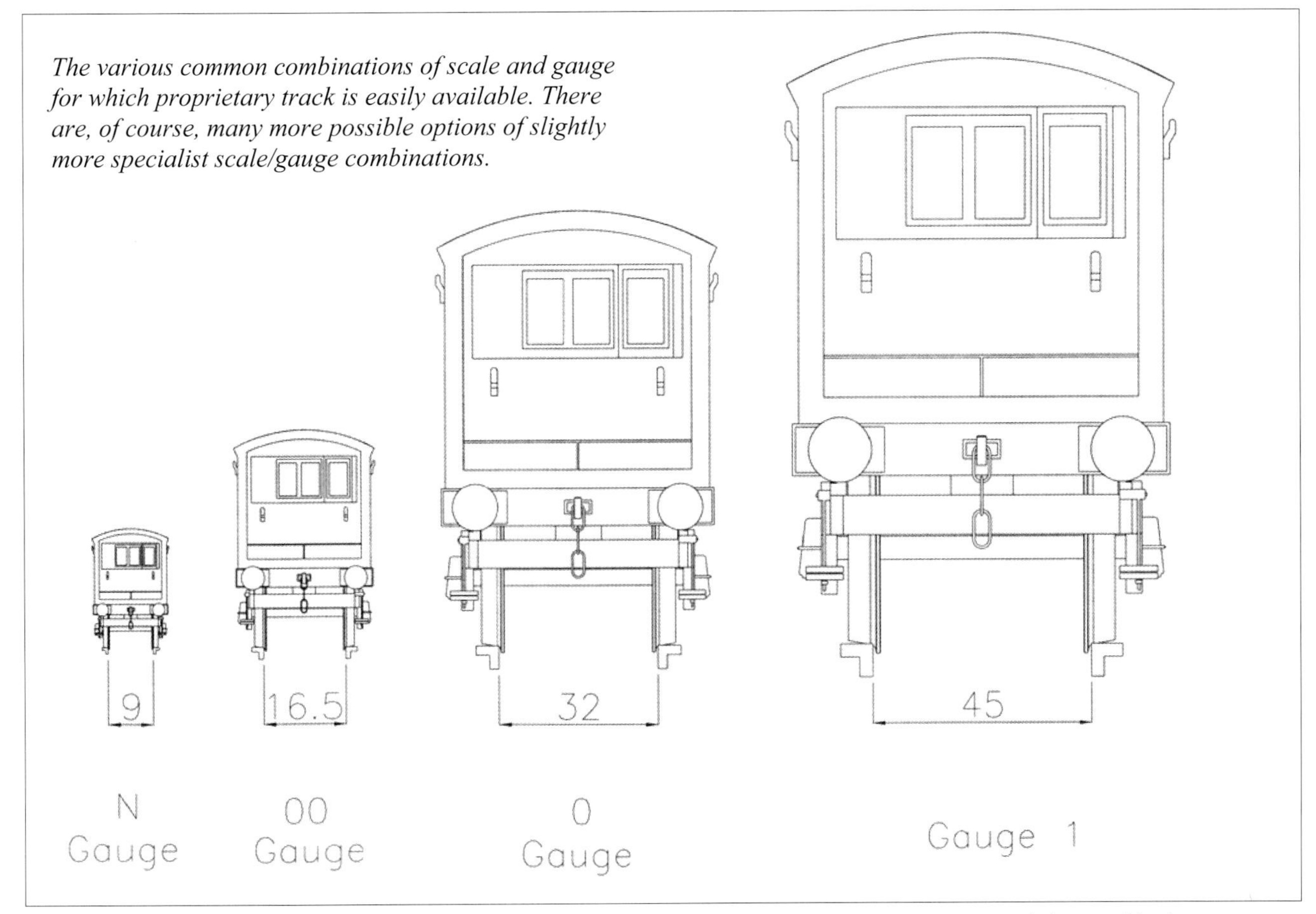

The various common combinations of scale and gauge for which proprietary track is easily available. There are, of course, many more possible options of slightly more specialist scale/gauge combinations.

THE SCALE AND GAUGE DECISION

Another of the important initial decisions which needs to be taken is to what scale and what gauge the line will be. In many cases this will already be decided – a modeller who has spent years constructing 0 gauge rolling stock is unlikely, on the move to a bigger house with a garden, to abandon it all and start out in N gauge.

I think most modellers are aware of the scales and gauges available – a glance at the PECO track range will display the majority of the various options and combinations. I have focused here on commercially easily available scales, as the amount of track and rolling stock and so on involved in the average garden railway is likely to act as a deterrent to anyone building a railway in a scale where they cannot buy track in 12 yard boxes.

STANDARD OR NARROW GAUGE?

As I have said before, this book has been written with modellers working primarily in gauges between about N and O in mind, and who are aiming to create a mainline in miniature in the garden rather than those wishing to build an SM-32 or G-45 narrow gauge empire, although smaller scale narrow gauge railways are included (0-16.5, 009). There are two clear divisions in the scale/gauge combinations frequently referred to - those with long names are narrow gauge ones and those with shorter, more succinct acronyms are for standard gauge modelling. Most people will have a fairly clear idea of what kind of modelling they want to indulge in, and the narrow/standard gauge decision will not be too difficult to make.

Narrow gauge railways can work very well outdoors. They fit happily into the outside surroundings, and I think can look better in the difficult-to-disguise 12 inches to a foot vegetation than standard gauge lines - possibly because we have a less clear mental picture of what the relative proportions of the gauge, width of stock and the surrounding structures and the landscape should be. Another advantage of mixing scales which I tend to exploit is that standard gauge rolling stock can be run on narrow gauge lines at a larger scale - and so should you be incapable, as am I, of settling on one railway, or indeed country, to model you can chop and change - I often run my French HO stock on my 0-16.5 line, whereas trying to run my Lynton and Barnstaple stock on an HO line would, I suspect, be less successful and rapidly demolish signals, buildings and bridges, and generally wreak all manner of havoc.

This mismatch of scales and gauges seems somehow a lot less obvious outdoors than it would be inside as there is already a significant discrepancy between the scale of the immediate environs of the line and any buildings or structures which are part of it. In the garden

A 7mm narrow gauge train heads up the bank to Grogley Junction. This kind of scale works very well outside, fitting in the garden surroundings to evoke memories of pictures of the early trains on the Ffestiniog or the Welsh Highland

the bigger picture becomes the focus – the prototypical speed, length of run and smoothness of curve holds the eye, and details such as the scale of the sleepers go virtually unnoticed.

Another advantage of the narrow gauge line in the garden is the possibility of modelling a complete system. Particularly within the British Isles we are used to narrow gauge lines a few miles long winding between a handful of stations with maybe an industry at one end and a port at the other. These lines can be re-produced in the garden in their entirety. It is very satisfying to plan, build and run a complete railway, and with two or three stations a railway can be created which is similar in terms of amount of stock and number of loops and sidings to the prototype, meaning prototypical operation naturally follows. Standard gauge lines, unless modelling light railways, tend to be linked into the national railway system, and this inherent prototypical operation never quite happens as you just don't have the rest of the country sending trains on down to you!

OUT AND BACK OR CONTINUOUS RUN?

I cannot urge you strongly enough to create a continuous run in your garden railway. I appreciate that operating short branch trains might be the principal reason behind the line, but as soon as you build a continuous run and recline in a garden chair to watch the trains go past you will, I swear, be a convert to the concept of circles of track. On those long summer evenings there is nothing more satisfying than watching an engine you built pulling a train you created faultlessly round a railway of your construction for hours. I have to confess I am generally too lazy to use the continuous run on my railway - the return loop at the end, built through the shed, is frankly a pain to put up and clean and there is sufficient operating potential without it. Whenever I do get it all working for a big operating session in the summer however I always notice how infinitely much more enjoyable it makes the railway to operate – it completely and utterly changes it from an awkward two station affair with a couple of return loops to a railway I am always quite impressed that I managed to build, with operational potential everywhere. The complete circuit not only allows you to sit back and enjoy the view but also makes concentrated operation considerably more enjoyable, allowing expresses to pass at speed through all the stations, with a few slow branch and goods trains slotted in between them, darting round the garden from goods loop to goods loop when a moment of let-up on the block instrument occurs.

Clearly if you are purely interested in running trains in the conventional sense of the test track principle, you will be well advised to create a circular run. At the very least I would recommend a half dog-bone shape or similar so you can send trains out of a station or storage sidings and they arrive back again without having to turn them at the other end, as the garden presents a real opportunity for enough track to just let trains run, and it would be a real shame to ignore this and fiddle about with two points and three yards of track.

The 'out and back' system, for want of a better term, is clearly more akin to the prototype and its main advantage is that it therefore forces more prototypical operation. It is a lot easier to wire than anything which

An example of the kind of prototypical curvature which can be modelled in the garden. With a train sweeping round a curve like this, the exact nature of the sleepers or ballast goes entirely unnoticed. This is the 200 chain radius curve just south of Woking on the Waterloo – Weymouth line in 1946, just after the laying of the then new flat bottomed rail. In 4mm scale this would be a 50m curve, which would look far better in the garden than straight track between stations.

looks like a return loop (oh how I dislike wiring return loops…) and it allows you to model terminus stations as well as the ubiquitous through station with a loop and a couple of sidings. In many respects the operational restrictions imposed at the termini of such a system - having to turn every train and send it out again - can create more operational interest than sending train after train round in the same direction, but then this operational interest can also be enjoyed in a continuous system; you just have to be a bit more self disciplined, and not keep sending the trains straight through!

GROUND LEVEL OR RAISED?

Traditionally, garden railways were often raised to a 'workbench' height (three feet or so) above the ground, running on wooden structures or on relatively high walls. There seems to have been a move recently however to ground level lines, especially amongst the larger scale live-steam movement, to capitalise on the aesthetic advantages enjoyed by these lines. If you are aiming to build a railway which blends into its surroundings there is no contest between a raised line and a ground level one – your knees will just have to bear the sacrifice.

With a ground level line the surrounding landscape can be mimicked by rockeries, rows of cottages, houses and indeed entire towns, which can be built beside the track as at Beckonscott in Buckinghamshire, and the whole layout will blend well into the garden. However, this aesthetic advantage and the slightly easier and cheaper construction are really the only advantage ground level lines can hold over raised lines, albeit a fairly significant one if you are aiming to create the full scenic landscape. Raised lines have a far greater number of advantages. They do not involve hours bent down on your knees and they are easier to clean and maintain. They do not suffer from the effects of the ground rotting a wooden trackbase in the same way that a ground level line does (although of course the posts will rot in time), and they are easier to wire as the wiring can be run simply under the boards.

That said, a bit of careful planning can provide a ground level line with some of these advantages. The rotting baseboard scenario can be avoided by building them on top of low brick walls, and the wiring can be run easily if careful thought is given to the provision of wiring ducts during construction.

If the line is to run from a station or from storage sidings in a shed, I would recommend a higher level to the running line as operating a station or set of sidings somewhere below knee height can get very tiring. The floor of a shed can always be lowered however to form an operating pit, and so gain the advantages of a waist-height station coupled with those of a ground level line outside.

The final decision on the height of line you create will depend significantly on the topography of your garden, and also how much time you are prepared to put in down on your hands and knees. It is important to remember that 'hands and knees time' is not only part of the construction of the line, but also of operating it in years to come. Of course if you are lucky enough to have a sloping garden you enjoy the best of both worlds, having a station in a shed or garage at perfect operating height with the lines running out and round the garden at ground level, or a course or two of bricks above.

One of the stations on my garden railway, supported on a low brick wall to the path to ease the amount of bending down required to operate it.

Survey pegs in action. Two inches square and about eighteen long, you can pick these up at a builders' merchant for a reasonable price and I get through almost as many as teabags. They come tanalised with a point ready cut, and can be used as here during surveying - and also to support trackbases, to hold up formwork for concreting, as a base for a point motor... the list is endless!

WORKING OUT WHAT YOU CAN FIT IN THE SPACE

While it is tempting to stand in the middle of the garden and describe, with a wave of the arm, a four-track main line cutting a graceful arc through the flower bed on the far side, the reality of what can be fitted in is often quite different and not apparent until either you start building or you get some kind of scale plan down on paper. For a lot of railway systems, laying some track out on the ground here and there and coming up with a rough plan will give you a sufficiently accurate idea of what you can fit in, particularly if you've got a bit of space to play with on either side. Certainly that's all I ever did – in fact you could argue that's more than I ever did, but then I have the odd rather tight corner in places to prove the wisdom of doing something more substantial.... If, however, you are looking to build a large system or you need a more accurate idea of where it will fit into the garden, it can be worth surveying the garden properly by triangulation. It is, after all, somewhat easier to tighten up the radius of a curve on an accurate plan by rubbing it out and adjusting the compass than by digging up a concrete foundation which strikes off through the neighbour's fence. Another advantage of planning things carefully on paper is that you can also sometimes see obvious improvements to a layout on a plan which you can't necessarily see so easily if you're balancing bits of track across flowerbeds trying to see what you can fit in. (There is a good description of surveying by triangulation in Site Surveying and Levelling, 2nd edition, by J Clancy. Butterworth-Heinmann Ltd ISBN 0 340 50547 8)

If you do go for the full survey and scale plan option once you have your plan of the garden I would advise making a few photocopies before you draw the track plan on; it is desperately annoying to have to set out the whole plan again!

Some consideration will also need to be applied to the vertical situation, which can be more difficult to interpret by eye. The situation in the vertical can be fairly easily checked with the aid of a spirit level and a long length of wood – you need something which won't bend, about three inches by one inch works well if turned on edge. You also need to pick a reference level – if the railway comes out of a shed or garage, this level can be used. If there is no obvious height to start at any point can be used, but it is worth making a note of where you started. Once you have a start point it is simply a matter of working round the garden in steps as long as the piece of wood, and measuring the change in height at each stage. I find that the easiest way to make the wood level is by packing up one end on a pile of bricks, tile or slate and then measuring at what height below the datum level each point on the survey lies. This can then be recorded on a plan or marked by a survey peg driven in to an appropriate height.

Whether to plan the whole line at ground level or to include gradients is a matter of personal choice and depends

Checking the vertical level. The pile of bricks and tile is used to level up the piece of timber and the height of this pile then measured for the plan, or a stake can be driven in to this height. The handful of sand on the ground at the bottom provides a level base to stop the pile of bricks falling over all the time and can be adjusted for precise variations smaller than the thickness of a bit of tile. These brick piers can be built on a much grander scale – I built some five feet high once piling bricks together dry to carry a level across a depression in the ground. You can use stakes instead if you don't have lots of spare bricks and bits of tile hanging around.

on the scale you are using and how much space you have. Certainly lines on gradients can add operational interest and in some cases they are unavoidable – this was the case with my railway, but I would have preferred to have it all on the level as the gradients do, undoubtedly, restrict the length of trains I can run – a restriction I would rather be without. There are no real hard and fast rules about how steep you can make gradients but I would recommend the flattest physically possible. A bit of experimentation with a plank, a few lengths of track and your least powerful engine will allow you to get an idea of what is practical. I have a gradient of 1:80 up to one of the stations to get the track high enough to get into the hut, which the trains run up fine, but the gradient of 1:24 which used to exist was so steep as to be unacceptably restricting, and I have since built something of a deviation to avoid it.

THE PHYSICAL LAYOUT

Once you have a plan of the garden you can easily work out the location of the railway, and it is at this stage, once you actually know the physical constraints on the layout, that the mental picture you will probably have developed of your line can be checked against what is practically possible.

Initially, rather than working out precise track layouts, it is easier and in a sense more important to get an overall picture of the line – where the runs of track will go and, critically, how the curves will all fit in. The minimum curve radii for various gauges are figures easily available from the societies dedicated to each gauge and, as with inside railway layouts, you go below these figures at your peril. While your stock might run round particularly tight curves it is important to bear in mind that it is likely that you will invite people to run their stock on your garden railway, and theirs is likely to run only on curves above the usual minimum radius.

I would recommend viewing things like paths and walls as moveable objects, to a degree, if you can get the whole household to agree on this fact. While I am not trying to claim that it is easy rebuilding walls or paths it is by no means impossible, and if you are investing a lot of time, effort and money into building a garden railway it is worth going the 'extra mile' and ending up with a railway that is truly a joy to operate, rather than one which you will constantly find yourself thinking 'Well, it's good, but if I had just done that...' If you are not keen on moving concrete paths yourself a builder will always do it – it's not a big job to him, and while he probably won't build level crossings to your specification he will happily leave a trench across the path for you to install a crossing later. Railways which have been truly built into the garden like this can look vastly better in the long run, blending in that much better.

As mentioned, the location of the stations is established at this early planning stage. They can of course be located outside or inside in a shed, garage or similar – this allows stock to be stored on the line which is undoubtedly an advantage, and it also allows the stations to be modelled in the usual 'inside modelling' manner. This allows significantly more detail to be included as it does not have to be weatherproof. Having stations inside also means you can have the power supply and possibly even the entire controls for the line permanently connected up in a weatherproof location, which is a lot easier than trying to make control panels removable through weatherproof connections outside. However it may be impossible to fit a station in inside through lack of available space - certainly this was the case with our garden.

It is also worth planning the location of the infrastructure around the railway, taking into account any drainage required and so on. This is especially true, in my experience, of the wiring runs. I never really considered these back in the beginning when I had four wires working the entire railway, but now, with over a mile of wire all over the place, I very much wish that I had. You need to consider the entire route of the wires from power supply

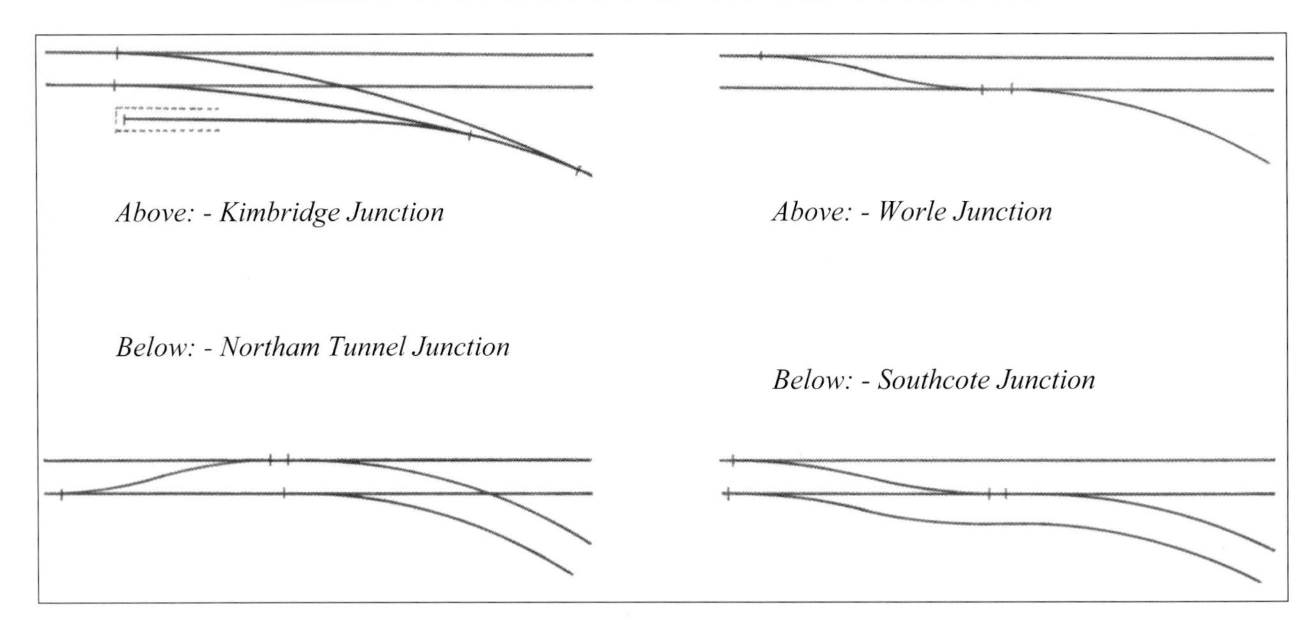

Some common railway junction track layouts. The two layouts on the left here represent the more historical approach, with a minimum of facing points and those on the right the more modern layouts, now that facing points locked by their motors are considered more acceptable. The top two layouts are for a single line joining a double track line and the lower two drawings are of a double track to double track junction.

right along the railway – if you are building a raised line on a wooden support they can easily be run under the baseboard; or with a high wall along the foot of it. Slightly more thought is required with ground level lines. At the planning stage you also need to work out where the wires will have to cross the track so you can leave a gap in the walls as you build them – I would leave half a brick out. I realise that that seems a bit extreme for a little bit of wire but it is amazing how these things mount up – the six wires to each of my point motors make a bundle of wiring about a quarter of an inch in diameter, and you quickly end up with thick wiring looms – especially with the heavy cable used outside.

THE TRACK LAYOUT ITSELF

Getting a good layout design is critical to the potential future enjoyment of operating a garden railway. In my opinion, modellers tend to try and re-invent the wheel when it comes to designing layouts. There are so many layouts in the real world and there is such diversity amongst them I have never quite understood why people don't just copy them, and to do so would be my advice to you. Most of the railway companies had their own favourite layouts and whole lines were often built to similar track plans. If you must invent layouts, to do it convincingly you need to follow the same mentality that the railway builders did when they came up with theirs. As a general rule, railway companies hated facing points as they could theoretically change under a train (hence facing point locks). The Great Western, for example, had a particularly paranoia about them, and had numerous country goods yards off loops with a difficult–to–maintain diamond in the other line, and the entire Settle and Carlisle was famously originally built without a single facing point.

Illustrated above are some very common junction layouts taken from real railway examples to get those creative thoughts running. When designing a layout it is essential to think it through from an operational point of view – to imagine driving trains round the layout, and see where you need sidings or loops. The best way, I find, to ensure you have a good layout is to draw it out and then work trains round it in your mind, or photocopy the design several times and draw the passage of the trains on with coloured pens to ensure there will be a flow of trains and that there are no obviously conflicting routes. It is a lot easier to work this out on paper than to build the layout and then have to make significant changes to it!

JUNCTIONS

In reality railway junctions are often miles from anywhere. Worting Junction, for example, on the LSWR south of Basingstoke, is an important junction of routes (the end of the 4-track section out of Waterloo and the division of the Southampton and Salisbury-Exeter routes westwards), but nowhere near a station. Meldon Junction on the side of Dartmoor is another good LSWR example, still today in a very isolated spot with only a couple of railway cottages within a mile of it, and there are almost as many examples of similarly isolated junctions as you would care to quote.

Rather than being included as part of a station, as so frequently seen inside, junctions can instead be situated

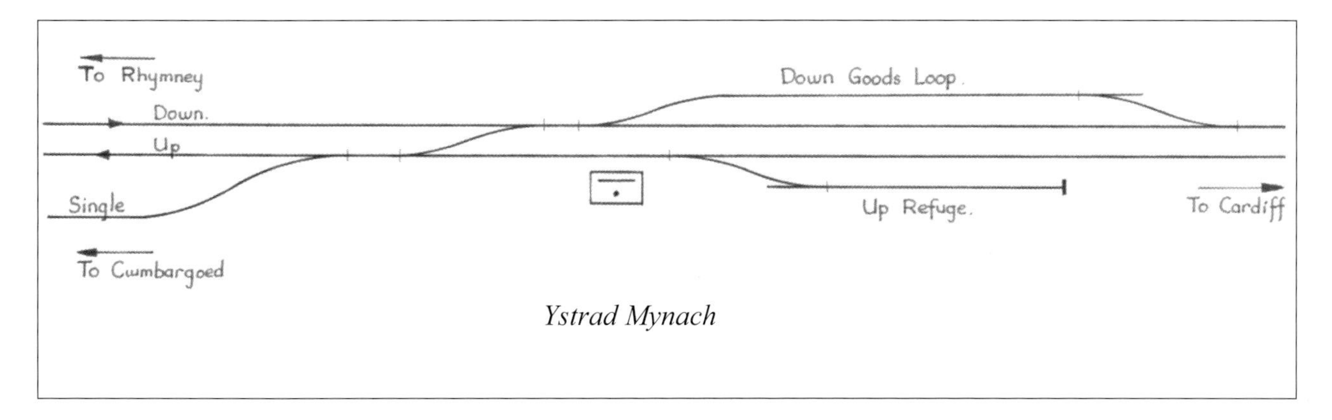

Ystrad Mynach, a typical Western region junction layout with crossover and lead junction, down goods loop and up relief siding. This is a layout which can be seen repeated all over the country.

in prototypically far-flung corners of the garden with only a lonely signal box in view, and it is little touches such as these which add realism to garden railways and vastly enhance the enjoyment derivable from operating them. When designing junctions, find a prototype example – the double junction was virtually universal, except on the Western Region of course, which just had to be different and used the crossover and lead junction fairly extensively, such as the example of Ystrad Mynach above.

LOOPS

Try and include as many loops as possible – while one in a station is good, why not one in the goods yard as well, to run round a train without having to move the whole thing to the station? Also, with all the space the garden offers, why not include a goods loop or two? These were a prolific feature of the railway network half a century ago, allowing slow moving freight to be passed, particularly on long stretches between stations, and there are many which still exist today. These become particularly appropriate to model railways in the garden, where there are often long stretches of track between operators. I had a goods loop for a long time about halfway between two stations, which proved incredibly useful not only for storing trains but also for making them up and passing them. Operators tended to use it for dropping a few wagons off trains which passed every now and again, and eventually picking the whole lot up with a pick-up freight, or just passing trains in section to confuse the operator at the other end. Eventually it got lifted as it was on a gradient and wagons kept running away: lesson one, build sidings and loops on the level. It was also in a difficult place to see from the controls, and wagons were frequently splitting the points as people changed them under the brake van. I wouldn't recommend locating things like the end of a loop out of sight of the operators, as knocks and bumps due to mis-timed changing of the points and unintentional loose shunting are, at the end of the day, borne by the stock that you have spent hours creating. The loop has since been reinstated on the level just behind the operator after a couple of years missing from the layout, such was the demand for its return.

LOCO FACILITIES

If you are intending to turn a lot of trains in a station, or change the engines on a high proportion of the trains which are passing through, you need to think carefully about the provision of sidings at either end. At least one siding, loop, or engine release needs to be available at either end of the station to get the leading engine out of the way of the train and to allow the new engine to set back out of a different road and onto the train. Such operations were common until fairly recently, and engine releases could also be found all over BR before the introduction of multiple units. These need to be installed in such a way that they can be accessed from all roads. The need for careful provision of engine facilities is especially true of termini, as explained below.

TERMINI

There are a large number of prototypical terminus arrangements out there which can be copied or slightly tweaked. Many of them are on too large a scale to be practically modelled by the bulk of us – sadly few of us can model Waterloo – but there are some smaller options. I have spent many happy hours operating the terminus layout shown overleaf, and I would very much recommend it as a layout for the end of a double track main line. Termini require serious planning if the end result is to be a layout which is easy and enjoyable to operate, and hours of frustration trying to turn trains around in a difficult layout can be easily avoided by a bit of careful thought at the planning stage. An afternoon spent watching the trains at Hardwick Central on the Great Cockcrow Railway (South London, 7¼" gauge) will be both enjoyable and instructive

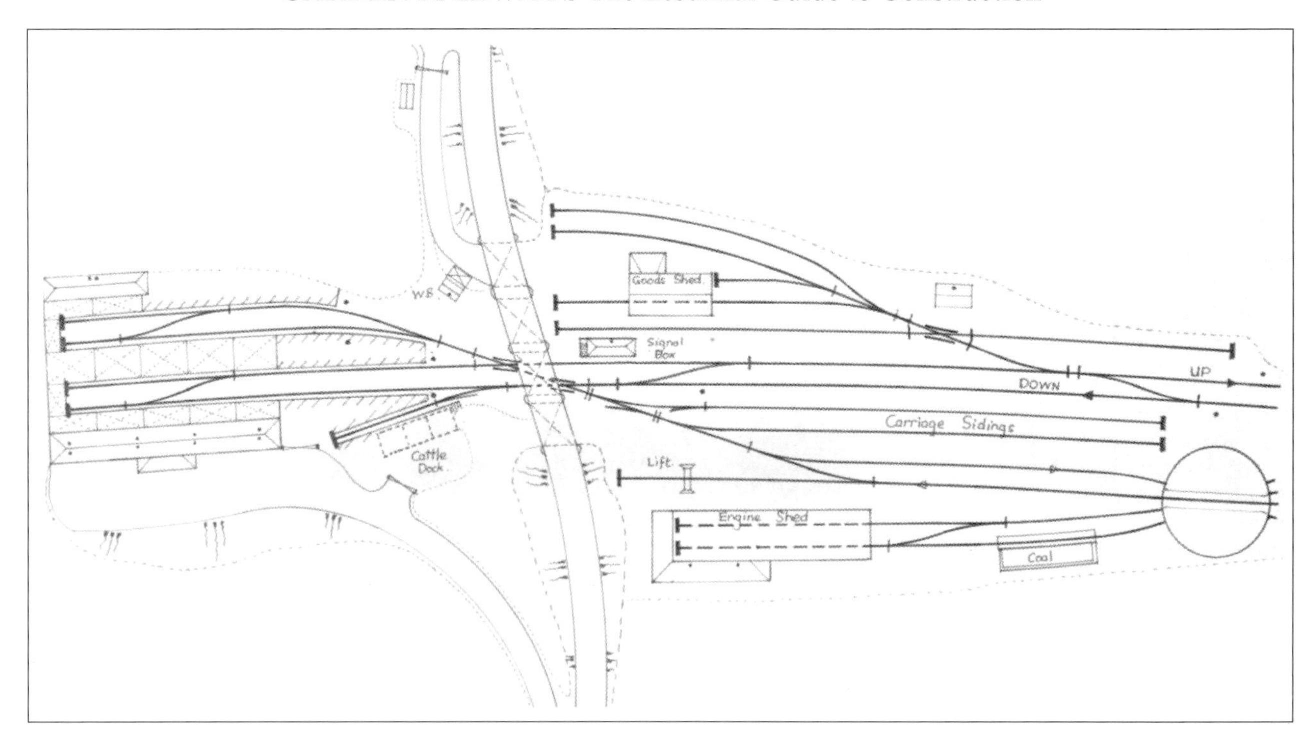

An enjoyable-to-operate terminus for a double track main line. Note the loco facilities easily accessible from any line, and the provision of crossovers on the platform roads for releasing an engine off the front of the train and allowing it to run up either road to the sheds. This layout also incorporates an extensive goods yard, cattle dock and carriage sidings yet is still surprisingly compact; it would for example fit perfectly into a standard length garage in OO with the main lines heading out through the wall at the end to wend round the garden and give the trains a chance to run at speed.

as to just how well a terminus can run if well thought out at the planning stage.

PLANNING THE CONSTRUCTION OF THE LINE

Constructing the line is, in my opinion, as enjoyable as operating it – and while I realise that not everyone out there will share this opinion, I suspect that those who do will, like me, prefer to build the line over many years than in one all-out effort. If you are going to build the layout section by section, then I recommend building the continuous run first, if you have one – the incentive to continue constructing the more complicated bits of the line once you can sit back and watch the trains go round from the comfort of a garden chair is considerable.

The length of the actual 'garden railway season' would also make it extremely difficult to build an entire line in one go, although I know some people do take this approach. If you intend to build the entire line at once then some careful planning will be required in terms of quantity surveying to ensure the right amount of timber or building materials turn up, depending on your chosen method of construction. While this approach requires significant capital outlay most building materials are cheaper in bulk, and savings can be made in comparison to the cost if the construction is spread over several years.

If you build the continuous run round the garden first and later come back to install loops, sidings and so on, it goes without saying that it is worth building the walls or timber trackbase to the shape required by the final layout, and then just laying a single line through the middle of it all. This is where the scale plan comes into its own, allowing you to establish the size of the base required. In some cases the levels dictate that a particular bit of the line must be built first – the first board out of a garage for example might be required to set the level of the rest of the line to; in which case, of course, you will have to lay this first. If you are going to get a builder in to rebuild walls, paths or patios around the route of the future railway it might be worth getting this done first to avoid potential damage by the builder to the sections already built at a later date.

While it probably appears from this section that a serious planning phase is needed before you can even consider anything running, in reality the actual planning required is not that arduous, most planning after all being something that can be slotted into odd minutes during the day as you stand at the bus stop or wait in the queue for lunch. I would however seriously recommend having some answers to at least most of the questions posed by the considerations above before construction commences in earnest outside. While an organic approach to planning does result in a workable railway, it may lead to more expense and be more time consuming than having a rough plan at the outset, and it is more difficult to build a line this way.

The conifers forming the backdrop to this photograph and the rocks on the right make a surprisingly convincing background, and it's easy to imagine the distant branch line terminus that the train is heading for - and in the garden, of course, the model could be in for a prototypically long run. Whilst the ability to run long express trains at speed is a definite advantage of garden railways and can bring many hours of viewing pleasure, it is equally enjoyable sometimes to run short branch line trains - and to watch them meandering slowly around the garden, just as the real thing used to meander slowly across England.

This is the sort of train that is absolutely perfectly suited to garden railways - a train so common on the prototype in its era yet so difficult to portray inside because it's just too long. This is Dennis Tillman's garden railway, demonstrating how very much better a gentle curve looks winding up the garden than a straight, and how a waist-high railway on a brick wall can be blended into the garden with careful planting to the front and rear.

2
THE MATERIALS INVOLVED

Construction of garden railways requires a completely different range of materials to those used in the construction of their indoor counterparts. Not only do they have to be weatherproof, but often a degree of building work is required to create a suitable base for the line, be it in brick or timber.

CONCRETE AND ITS CONSTITUENT PARTS

Concrete is probably the most versatile of building materials. It is strong in compression, relatively cheap, easily obtainable and easy to work with, and can be made to fit any situation. It is simply mortar and coarse aggregate as shown below. It is a very old material (the Romans are often credited with its discovery) but also very complicated, and cement chemistry is not fully understood to this day. The mortar, be it used for bricklaying, making concrete or creating buildings in the garden, is a mixture of sand and cement in the appropriate ratios.

Cement comes from the clinker of heated clay and limestone or similar materials and is usually brought as OPC (Ordinary Portland Cement) in 25kg paper bags. It has a rapid reaction with water and also eventually goes off in air - a half bag kept in a shed over the winter will be hard by the next spring purely by reacting with air borne moisture. It is worth thinking carefully about how much cement you are going to use as it is very space-consuming when stored in a suitably dry place such as inside a garage. Unlike most materials, it is usually no cheaper to buy in bulk and the only unit available is 25kg. OPC (The standard blue circle cement) is purely a regularly updated standard to which all cement manufacturers must adhere: it does not all come from a big hole near Weymouth.

The coarse aggregate is the stone part, and for our purposes the most useful size is 20mm or so which is about right for foundation concrete. If some fine concrete is needed for a viaduct or similar perfectly good concrete can be mixed using 10mm aggregate – occasionally called pea shingle - it will just be slightly more expensive.

I would very much recommend getting bulk materials – sand and aggregate – from a quarry, sandpit or bulk aggregate supplier if you have space to store it, and get them to deliver it. It will come in a lorry and they will either tip it on the drive, which is cheaper, or crane it off the lorry in bulk bags.

Sand pits and quarries vary in the unit in which they sell things - it is usually either by ton or by cubic yard, and can vary from item to item in one quarry. A ton is often what comes in a bulk bag and loose tipped material is often sold by the cubic yard. There are 27 cubic feet of material in a cubic yard, or about eight or nine good wheelbarrow loads. A cubic yard is similar enough to a cubic metre, and a tonne roughly equivalent to a ton in the conversion table overleaf. If you are mixing up foundation concrete around 10:1 you'll need about 75kg of cement for every ton of aggregate, or about three bags. Similarly, a 25kg bag of sand is about five shovel loads, and if mixing mortar from these bags I just count the bags I put in the mixer and add a shovel full of cement for each.

If you are looking to get material tipped and move it in one day you can move (as a very rough average) about eight tons or five cubic yards in a day without totally tiring yourself out, and, should you be using them, there is a definite art to emptying ton bags. My preferred technique is to get a good shovel and stand on top of the stuff and dig it out from underneath you. You can usually drag them, but only when they have about three cubic feet left in them

The constituent parts of concrete. Cement on the left, sand on the right and coarse aggregate, in this case broken up old concrete which is fine for a rough foundation concrete, on the bottom.

There is a conversion table below, which gives values to convert between and work with these quantities.

Commodity	1 tonne in m^3 (i.e. volume of 1 tonne)	1 m^3 in tonnes (i.e. weight of 1 m^3)
Ballast	0.6	1.6
Cement	0.7	1.4
Clay	0.5	1.9
Dry sand	0.6	1.6
Loose gravel	0.6	1.6
Loose soil	0.7	1.4

It is very uneconomical to buy lots of 25kg bags from a DIY store. As an example (again very roughly) a cubic yard of sand will cost about £20 tipped (plus delivery), £40 in a ton bag (plus delivery) and about £100 in 25kg bags. Although the prices are rough and will unfortunately go up, the proportions will remain similar. In most circumstances the unit in which you buy will be dependent on the storage available to you, but buy in the biggest bulk you can accommodate to keep the price as painless as possible, even to the extent that the rate of delivered sand will be a lot cheaper per ton for, say, four tons delivered at once than if you are asking the suppliers to drive out to you with half a ton on a lorry on eight separate occasions. If a whole railway is planned for construction in one go I would recommend digging all the foundation trenches, hiring a mixer, buying the aggregate to turn up on a Saturday and doing it all in a day as it will save you a great deal of money and it's a lot easier to get into the swing of concreting and do it all in one go than to keep starting and stopping.

Builders' merchants will often sell you the ton bags of material along with all the other items you will need - OPC (not the publisher), wood for levelling posts, bricks – and it can all be delivered to site in one go, the smaller items usually tucked inside the top of the bags to defeat you as you try to check off the delivery sheet. This means if you are going for one big weekend of construction you won't need to store anything beforehand. It will nearly always look too much when the materials arrive – have faith in your calculations however; it will probably be too little when it actually goes in the hole. Try and find a relatively local builders' merchant for materials and get to know them. The chain builders' merchants are not at all bad for price, especially in comparison with DIY stores.

The mortar which goes between the stones in concrete is a mixture of sand and cement. Bricklaying mortar is made with builders' sand which is the softish yellow sand whereas the mortar in concrete is usually made up with sharp sand or grit sand – this is coarser than building sand, but then for concrete it doesn't need to be particularly fine.

It's worth trying, at least, to keep sand dry if you are going to be hand mixing it in small quantities for making things like model buildings as it sticks together when wet which makes mixing it well significantly more difficult and tiring to achieve. If you're buying 25kg bags simply tuck the top of the bag down and put half a brick on top to stop it flapping round in the wind and the sand will be kept good and dry.

OTHER BULK MATERIALS

Other bulk materials particularly useful to the garden railway builder include hardcore and scalpings, the latter shown below. Hardcore can be bought easily if not acquired by a bit of careful questioning in the bar of the local for free. If you buy it in it is usually crushed concrete – you can generally either buy it rough in big, heavy lumps or, as I prefer, crushed from three inch lumps down to dust. Because concrete crushed in this way contains both big lumps of concrete and everything else in size order down to sand it all locks together to create a good, solid surface when you lay it and compact it together well. It is fantastic for bulk fill but quite unsightly – it is often just crushed houses so bits of sockets and building site junk make it into

Three inch to dust crushed concrete hardcore underlies this area of made ground, but a layer of scalpings finishes off the top in a far more aesthetically pleasing manner. The low wall on the right is of reclaimed bricks – I much prefer the variation in their size and consequently less-than-perfect result to that of modern mass-produced bricks. Now wouldn't a 28XX with fifty or so grubby private owner wagons look good on that wall...?

the finished (very cheap) product and you can't really use it where it will be seen, although it is useful stuff for bringing levels up under patios or sheds to where you want them. If you are filling a large visible area, for example behind a wall with the railway on top, I would recommend crushed hardcore for the majority of the fill and then blinding the top 150mm off with a layer of scalpings, if you can get them. Scalpings are a mixture of crushed limestone and clay which compacts well, but also looks pleasing to the eye, especially after it has rained and the limestone stands out.

BRICKS

There are three distinct types of brick - facing, common, and engineering. Facing bricks are the most common and have a hard sandy finish on three sides which makes them capable of resisting the weather as long as they are laid with the facing edge outwards. If any of the other edges are exposed, the weather will get into the brick and eventually destroy it. Common bricks are the cheapest but only suitable really for indoor work as they will fall apart outside due to their lack of a weather-resistant face. Engineering bricks are much more solid and dense and will not absorb water, which makes them suitable for underground work such as foundations and manholes. In these situations of constant immersion normal facing or common bricks will absorb far too much water and fall apart. The red bricks with three holes are partial engineering bricks – well suited to manhole work and so on. These are very cheap but not very attractive; the blue solid engineering bricks are better for locations where they will be on display such as the top of a wall.

Beyond these there are many variations; useful to the garden railway builder are older bricks, which look more attractive and are generally suitable for laying with any face exposed to the weather, as they were made in a completely different way to modern bricks.

The absorption of water is a very important thing to bear in mind when dealing with bricks. It is what allows them to stick together and also what will destroy them if they are used in the wrong way. If a non-facing edge is left open to the rain eventually the bricks will absorb a huge amount of it and as the water freezes it will push the bricks apart from the inside. This is why a row of transverse bricks with a facing edge on top, called sleeper bricks, must be laid on top of all brick walls to provide a weatherproof top. If this step is missed the result, after a few years, is that shown below.

It is also possible to use engineering bricks for a row on top of the wall as mentioned above, but these are a lot more expensive. A ring of older bricks along the top of

Old reclaimed, partial engineering and full engineering bricks.

The need for sleeper bricks. These modern bricks have completely disintegrated through incorrect use – the top row should be either of solid engineering bricks or of bricks laid on edge to keep the weather out.

the wall (if the rest of the wall is not built of them) is a good substitute, as they are slightly harder all round and have no true facing edge. In purely decorative work tile or similar can be laid on top of the wall, but this is not a very practical idea if a railway is to be built on top of this. I would not rely (having seen it go wrong) on a piece of felt under the track as ballast to also keep the weather out with modern bricks – it might work for a few years but eventually they will disintegrate under the track.

FINDING THE RIGHT BRICK

There are literally hundreds of individual types of brick, as a visit to a builders' merchant will demonstrate. It is usually desirable, with all this potential variation, to try and match the bricks used in any new work with bricks which are already used on the property, for example to the bricks the house is made of. The best way to establish what brick is used in a house is to look around the garden as most builders leave a few bricks behind which get incorporated into garden projects. If these are moveable it is often easiest to take one to the brick merchants and ask their advice or look round their yard. Brick companies, for example LBC (London Brick Co) tend to stamp their name in the frog (depression under the brick) which aids the searching process a little.

In contrast with widely available bricks like LBC commons there are also a lot of 'specials', which are slightly out of the ordinary and can work better (aesthetically) in some situations. These however are likely to only be available if bought in bulk, usually in a whole pallet – a quantity which can range from 380 to 600 bricks per pallet. More common bricks, such as LBCs, can usually be brought from a builders' merchants in any reasonable number (in units of ten or so), although they usually only want to deliver big quantities in the range of about 350 or above. I prefer using reclaimed old bricks purely from an appearance point of view (although they are usually a bit more durable too). These can be brought from reclamation yards – be warned however, they are more expensive. Whereas a thousand modern facing bricks might cost you in the region of £300 (2004), a thousand reclaimed bricks will cost you nearer to £600.

TIMBER

Most garden railways incorporate a considerable amount of timber in their construction – this is especially true if you intend to raise the trackbase off the ground on a timber supporting structure, but even low level lines on brick walls often require a timber trackbase. Clearly it is desirable to minimise the amount of timber employed as it will rot over time, but personally I think the significantly enhanced running that results from laying track on a wooden trackbase more than repays the extra outlay on decent timber, and even the expense and effort involved in replacing a section of trackbase should it deteriorate over time.

The timber employed will need to be significantly more weather resistant than the thin ply or chipboard used inside. Personally I tend to use ¾ inch (18mm) ply for curves, junctions and awkward bits outside, an example of which is shown below. Marine ply, with waterproof glue and hardwood veneers, is best but incredibly expensive, and shuttering ply, designed for use in retaining and forming wet concrete on large construction sites, is a good alternative. The best approach to buying wood is to get the best you can afford, which is true for either plywood or for sections.

For long straight stretches I find it easier to use pre-sawn strip wood. A piece of timber around three inches by one (75mm by 25mm) is ideal for a single track in any scale up to 7mm to a foot. When it comes to sections of wood for supporting structures and for track bases, again, buy the best you can afford. The ideal approach is to use hardwood from a timber merchant, but this again is very expensive. A perfectly sound structure can be built up out of sawn softwood either tanalised or creosoted which should last for many years. Timber like this can be bought from the same builders' merchants as the bulk sand and aggregate – I would recommend this source over DIY stores as the timber is usually better suited to a life outdoors.

A ¾" ply track base for a junction location.

3

CONSTRUCTING THE BASE

Critical to successful and enjoyable operation of a garden railway is well laid track which does not constantly cause derailments, and which stands up to the rigours of the weather and being outside over long periods of time. To achieve this, it is essential that a strong and durable base is built for the line. I very much recommend a wooden base to lay the track itself on, as this allows the alignment and vertical level of the track to be finely adjusted and fixed once right.

It is possible to lay the track on the top of a brick or block wall and to tie it down loosely with wire mortared in the joints, but it is difficult to accurately control the alignment this way. In time the track straightens out at the joints on curved sections, giving a series of corners as opposed to the nice smooth curves the garden lends itself to, and the level of the track is dependant on accurately laid bricks, which even the best of bricklayers would find hard to lay to the millimetre tolerances necessary for good running in, say, N gauge. The cross-level of the bricks usually also changes slightly with every new brick, resulting in a twist every nine inches, which is a recipe for disaster. A wooden trackbase solves both of these problems allowing the track to be nailed down to give good alignment and by spanning over many bricks to prevent sudden changes in cross-level.

To support this wooden trackbase there are two main options. Either a wall can be built up, or a wooden supporting structure built. This is the same for both ground-level or raised lines – with ground level lines you will need something to support the track base and hold it slightly off the ground or it will rot very quickly.

This section will first deal with walling and then with wooden supporting structures. These two approaches by no means cover all the possibilities for supporting the track - as ever with garden railways, there are many other options available. Just concreting in a trench and screwing a wooden track base to this, for example, will provide a perfectly good trackbase for any garden railway.

FOUNDATIONS

Foundations are critical to garden railways and, I feel, often overlooked and misunderstood. There are few building applications where the alignment and long term stability of the top of a wall are more important than when there is a line of track on it, yet decent foundations, which would ensure good alignment and resistance to twisting of the wall, are hardly ever installed.

There is no real need for concrete foundations to support the physical weight of the wall in an average low level garden railway where there are four or so courses of brick; they could be laid straight on the surface of the ground. Proper foundations are however required to stop the wall tilting away from the vertical or moving longitudinally. These movements both arise from one of the most important lessons that the garden railway builder must learn – topsoil moves. It is terrible material to build anything on, and walls founded on it will undoubtedly

A wooden supporting structure for a low level trackbase. This is built from two inch square survey pegs and three inch by one inch rough sawn timber, and is very quick and easy to construct, the downside being that it will never be as solid or as permanent as a brick wall. Personally I wouldn't build it a lot higher than a foot or so before changing to three inch square posts as the two inch variety are not that stable in the ground and, for long term trouble free running, the whole needs to be rock solid.

crack, move and generally fall apart after the first winter. The main reason for this movement, and consequent destruction of walls built on top of it, is that it absorbs large volumes of water in the winter, causing it to swell, and then loses it all in the summer, shrinking again. If you take one lesson from this book, I hope it is to never build walls straight on the ground surface. Derailments are guaranteed if you do. Beyond this critical truth, it is difficult to state cut and dried rules for building foundations. Every situation is different. If you live in Hampshire and have chalk 100mm down in your garden, digging down to this and then building the wall off it will provide a foundation which will last forever. If, however, you live in an area with 200mm of topsoil or so and then clay, which is quite commonly found in the UK, a different arrangement is necessary.

The key is not to build on the topsoil – you need to get down to the subsoil – the clay underneath. There are then two main options. You can concrete about 150mm in the bottom of the hole on the subsoil and then build the wall up to ground level underground. If you do this I would advocate a line of concrete blocks below ground as they are cheaper than any other option, each course taking up three courses of bricks in height with significantly less effort and expense than actually laying the bricks. The other main option is to concrete right up to the surface – it depends really on how much the concrete is costing you and how much you like block-laying in a hole. If you go for the mass concrete option it does not need to be especially good concrete: 10:1 ballast to cement will be fine once it has had a good amount of time (a week or so) to gain strength, and you can also throw some hardcore in with the concrete to bulk it out a bit if you have a lot around. The mass concrete option, as shown overleaf, is simpler where you are aiming to build a double skin wall on top, and building up the foundation with a ring of blocks is generally simpler if you are going to put a single skin wall on top.

If it is a very long way down to anything firm in your garden then you are not going to be very inspired by the concept of digging down a disproportionately long way to put a small wall on top. Instead I would recommend digging a trench a foot (300mm) or so deep, putting some hardcore in the bottom and ramming it down well and then concreting over the top with 150mm or so of stronger concrete - 5:1 or similar. This will act to spread the load of the wall out better over softer bits of ground.

Marking out foundations can be quite difficult for railways, as they have to be more or less exactly in the right place. Stringlines are a good start as it is easy to see where they are going for straight foundations. A couple of stout pegs or canes and you are away. It is fairly awkward to dig a trench around a stringline however, so it is worth transferring the line to the ground once it has been set up. An easy way to do this is with building sand - with the stringline still set up drop some dry sand over it from just above it and where it lands will give you a good indication of where to dig. If it is dry sand it will fall either side of the string giving you a strip devoid of sand which is the exact point of the line.

For curves a tape or string can be used wrapped around a post at the centre of the arc, a number of points on the curve can be marked with sticks or sand and the rest 'eyed-in' between them. This is adequate for the purposes of setting out the trench. If it is not possible to get to the centre of the curve with a string a template can be cut to the right radius and used to set out. This, however, is not ideal as it is difficult to align each section of the curve with the previous, and a series of curves at different tangents to each other often results.

Setting up strings. In this case the far end is wrapped around a brick on the wall in the distance, which works well as you can lean the brick backwards slightly to keep the string taught. You can see the sand on the ground where the stringline has been transferred down for the purposes of digging the trench. There was a corner in the wall here a couple of yards beyond the post towards the wall – it is a good idea to have some overlap to the post to give you room to work.

Relative volumes of materials in concrete.

	Cement	Course aggregate	Fine (10mm) aggregate	Sharp sand	Building sand
Foundation concrete	1	3		2	
Fine concrete for casting arch bridges	1		2	2	
Bricklaying mortar	1				4
General mix for 'stonework' (retaining walls, walls of buildings etc.)	1			3	1

Once the line for the trench has been set out it can be dug. A mattock is my preferred tool for trenching – a pick-axe like tool with a large flat blade at one end for digging and a pick-like point at the other which allows you to easily break up anything that gets in the way. A fork is another good tool. By far the easiest way to dig a trench is to get in it and break it out towards you – even for small trenches. It is a lot more difficult to dig something like this out if you are stood on the sidelines.

Once the trench has been dug you need to put some pegs in the bottom to give some indication, once the hole is full of concrete, of what level it needs tamping down to. Putting these level pegs in is essentially the reverse of the process used to survey the ground in the first place. Once you've got the first one in to the right height you can just use a long piece of wood and a level to set the tops of the rest of them at the same height. It is useful if they go in square and level on top as this makes it a lot easier to strike the concrete off later.

These pegs can be pretty much of any spare timber, something about two inches square is good as anything much smaller tends to get difficult to spot once the whole area is full of concrete. The survey pegs which were shown previously are ideal. If you are cutting your own they need to have some kind of point on the bottom or it will be very difficult to get them in the ground straight. Either cut the end to a V or a proper four sided point, using the latter for more compact soil as they are a lot easier to get in.

If you are planning to build a wall a few courses high on top of this foundation you are most probably thinking foundations such as those above are ridiculously over-engineered, but you cut the scale of the foundations down at your peril. If they end up being inadequate you have to take the entire railway apart to do anything about it. The ground is nothing like as stable as you might believe until you build a precise line of tiny rails across it and watch them move.

CONCRETE

Concrete is synonymous with foundation construction. It is easy to make and can be cast to any shape – this makes it ideal to underpin a wall with. In most cases the garden railway builder will be measuring the constituent parts of concrete out by volume – a shovel load being the quantity most often used. The mixes quoted above are, in my experience, most useful. Everything is quoted relative to one part of cement.

The actual physical mixing is best achieved by a concrete mixer. If you don't have one or a friend with one you can borrow and you are doing a big pour I would recommend hiring one. They are not expensive on just a 'weekend hire' basis – at 2004 prices you should get change from £40 including delivery - and make life a great deal easier. The quantities of material required in foundation building are surprisingly large - a cubic yard of concrete would require about two tons of material moved once you include the cement and water and such things, and would equate to about a five metre length of foundation for a nine foot wall, which isn't all that long in the garden. If you are constructing an entire garden railway from scratch, by far the easiest way to tackle the potentially daunting construction work involved in building the foundations is with a mixer, a wheelbarrow, an eager helper and a weekend free from other commitments, with lots of pre-dug trenches ready for concrete first thing on Saturday morning, and level pegs set and ready to use.

If you are planning on mixing a lot of concrete in one go it is worth getting a bit organised on the location of the piles of aggregate when they are delivered and thinking out where the mixer will go – this makes life significantly

Planned laying out of the mixer, aggregate, water supply and so on will make mixing significantly easier. In this photo the aggregate is on the left about the right distance away for shovelling, the water supply is on hand (foreground) with a hose from a distant tap running at a carefully set trickle, the electricity supply has been sorted out and the cement is in a handy place for access to the drum. The essential ingredient that is washing up liquid is on top of the cement. On the left, in the sand, is a long handled Cornish shovel – ideal for moving sand and other dry, loose materials

easier when it comes to the physical mixing.

Mixers come in lots of different shapes and sizes – a small electric one is perfectly adequate simply because that is about all that will fit in a barrow. If you are hiring and you don't have a site box transformer, make sure you specify a 240V mixer or you might get a 110V one which won't, obviously, be a lot of good! Also check you get left a pin to hold the legs together – I have tried many times to find a way to get round a lack of one of these on site, never particularly successfully.

To get a good, fluid mix you want to add some sort of plasiciser in – you can use those sold for the purpose in builders' merchants, but I have to confess to usually using washing up liquid, which works just as well. You only need a few drops in a bucket of water. To physically mix the concrete, get the mixer going, put about half a builders' bucket of water in and then add the sand/ ballast in, adding the cement in last or it will stick to the drum. I usually put in about 10 or 12 shovels of sand or ballast and then however much cement is needed to make up the required mix. Top up what will probably be quite a dry mix with water until it looks right, using as a very rough guide another half a bucket or so. It's difficult to define 'when it looks right', but after doing it a few times you'll come to recognise the telltale signs. When you can see the back of the drum, when it is all the same colour and it just flows around the inside of the mixer but is still solid enough to get pulled up by the mixing slats on the inside of the drum, it's there. Once mixed, pour it into a barrow with the drum still turning and wheel it to where it is required. Don't overfill the wheelbarrows as they are fairly difficult to manoeuvre and a mistake means three cubic feet of concrete setting all over the garden, which is hell to move.

The mixer will need cleaning out after use. The old way is to get a few half bricks, throw them in with some water and let the whole lot mix for a while, the bricks getting everything out of the drum, after which the water can be dumped in a not too obvious place. This only really works well with softer older bricks however; more modern bricks are more brittle and tend to break in the drum. A useful tool if you have one is a hose with an adjustable spray on the end which can be turned off by a trigger grip attachment, this saves a lot of water being lost all over the garden. Invariably you will not make it back to the tap in time to turn off a conventional hose.

Once you have a barrow of concrete (it's a lot easier to do than to explain) you can get to the business of actually placing the concrete. The concrete can be poured directly from the barrow into the trench, and then persuaded in the right direction and compacted with a shovel vibrated up and down for a few seconds until the air bubbles stop rising to the surface. A rough finish is desirable on top as otherwise the mortar will not adhere

Steps formed in a concrete footing by pushing a couple of old bricks into the footing end-on. A board across the trench would make an equally good alternative. The two bricks are to hold the concrete back and create a step to cater for the changing level of the falling ground, and have been installed a planned number of full brick lengths from the end of the wall – cutting bricks is prone to going wrong and consequently can get expensive, and is therefore best avoided.

well when it comes to laying the bricks on top. The easiest way to achieve this is to use a tamper bar to compact the top surface of the concrete - ideally this should be a long straight bit of timber which is jiggled up and down over the surface of the concrete (two people make this job a lot easier). If trying to create a flat topped slab it is a lot better to use a wooden tamping bar than a float as if a float is drawn over the surface it will bring all the water to the surface, which means you get a very weak top to the concrete.

If a sloping site is being used it is perfectly practical to cast steps in the concrete to allow for the slope, using something like a board or a couple of old bricks end-on in the concrete to create the actual step. It is desirable to plan the location of the steps so they are a number of full bricks from the beginning of the wall otherwise bricks will have to be cut around the step - which is by no means an impossible feat, but is tricky, and with a little planning can be avoided. A couple of bricks pushed into wet concrete to form a step in the footing can be seen in the illustration on the previous page.

It is not very practical to try and get the concrete to stand above the ground level as it will slump as it dries and generally not be a success. It is also important that the concrete does not dry out too quickly or it will not set properly. If it looks like the concrete is drying out very rapidly, wet the surface with a hose on a fine setting or it will become very weak. It is always possible to hand mix concrete; in fact if only a small amount of mix is needed this is the only practical way. A large squareish board is needed on which the dry ingredients can be mixed until blended, a suitable amount of water can then be added and the whole mixed. You can also mix it in a bucket, and the same goes for mortar, but this does not really qualify in any sense as an easy way to do it. If you are going to use a bucket to mix mortar, put the sand in first, then the cement on top with a drop of washing up liquid, and with a pointing trowel pull the sand up through to mix it all together dry, finally adding the water.

I wouldn't recommend concreting if there is anything sharper than a very slight frost, and if you do work in these conditions you will need to cover the setting concrete with a board or bit of old sacking, and add a bit of frost-proofer to the water in the mix. Get a bottle of Wintamix in a builders' merchants and follow the instructions.

WALLING

There are two main types of walling in which we are interested – that made from brick and that made from block. Stone walling uses more or less the same techniques and is, of course, more common in some areas of the country. The type of walling used is another area where there is great variation from place to place in terms of which method is most commonly used, for example in the clay-rich South East virtually all walling is brick whereas in the predominately stone South West far more block and stone walling is found. In my opinion, bricks look slightly nicer than blocks and have the advantage of making a truly waterproof wall unlike blocks, but for this they do work out more expensive. Composite walls also make nice features, for example brick walls with flint or stone infill. These, like stone walling, rely on the same techniques and if you can understand brick walling you can definitely manage flint or stone. The only difference with flint is that lime mortar should be used – unhydrated lime can be brought in most builders' merchants, but be aware that it is fairly aggressive and you should wear gloves and safety

Different brick bonds. At the top a four and a half inch stretcher bond wall, below it nine inch Flemish and English bond walls. The corners are the tricky bits with the bottom two – you need to cut down some Queens Closures (the little quarter bricks) – this is quite easy with older bricks and can be achieved using either chisel or brickie's hammer, but you're really into angle grinder/disc saw territory with modern brittle bricks. If in doubt about how to construct a corner build it up dry to get the structure in your mind and then attack it with some mortar – once you've got it you'll understand forever, but it can be difficult to imagine. Certainly it took me a few corners to get it right

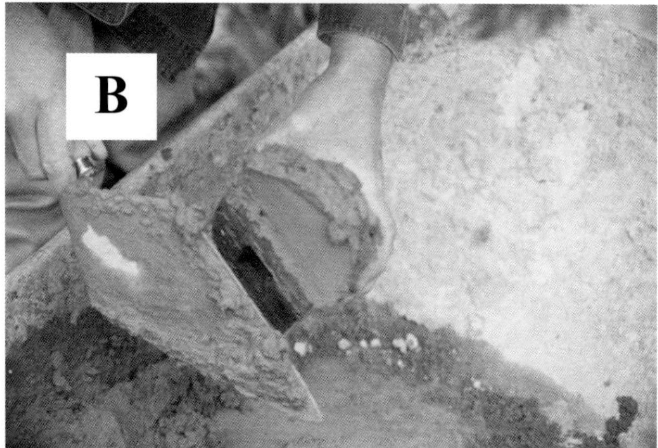

glasses when using it. In the section below, brick walling is explained first and then block walling.

BRICK WALLING

There are a few specialist terms associated with bricklaying as it is an empirical art which has evolved over many centuries and can be confusing at first. The 'frog' is the depression under the brick which makes it slightly lighter and also allows a good physical connection when in the wall as the mortar effectively locks into this and then goes hard. There are 'facing edges' on three sides of a facing brick to keep out the moisture; these are the hard sandy edges – normally two ends and a side. Bricks can be laid with either a long or a short side in the face of the wall – if laid lengthways they are referred to as 'stretchers' and if laid head-on they are referred to as 'headers'. There are a number of different brick bonds which can be used – stretcher bond gives a good four and a half inch wide wall whereas the other two types of bond shown here, Flemish and English bond, give good nine inch walls. The precise type of bond used is not particularly important and from an aesthetic point of view should, like the brick type, be matched to the house or surrounding existing buildings. Double track in 00 gauge or similar will happily fit on a nine inch wall, whereas a stretcher bond wall is ideal for a single track in anything up to and including '0' gauge.

An option for saving bricks (and money) is to construct a double-skin wall with blocks on the back and bricks on the front, preferably tied together with butterfly ties or something similar. Although this is technically slightly less strong than a Flemish bond wall it is more than sufficiently strong for garden railway applications. If this is being built in the garden of a house which is in Flemish bond things can be kept looking 'right' by putting half-bricks in the outer skin to give the impression of the headers in Flemish bond.

STRETCHER WALL BONDING

Straight stretcher bond walling is by far the easiest type of walling, and a pile of bricks and a good supply of

A - Laying the horizontal bed of mortar for a course of block. This is slightly tricky down a trench, but as long as there is some all over and a good bit at the front to give a nice edge to point above ground level it's not critical whether it looks pretty or not.

B - Placing the mortar on the end of the brick before laying it, referred to sometimes as 'buttering up the perpend'.

C – Knocking a brick down into the bed with a lump hammer.

D - Filling in between blocks with the aid of a backing board. In a trench like this a pointing trowel is slightly easier to work with.

mortar in a wheelbarrow can fairly quickly be transformed into a wall which is a simple and, I find, very enjoyable task. A stringline can be a useful tool to get the alignment of the wall good and straight if you aren't going for the sweeping curves gardens were invented to incorporate – you can use it to check the level of the bricks as well, but to be honest I find it easier just to use a long level.

The actual laying process is very simple, and while the first few bricks of the day might be a bit slow you very quickly get into the rhythm of it. Firstly a pyramid shaped line of mortar in the middle of the wall is spread out slightly and a brick taken to be laid on top. It is easiest to put the mortar on the end first rather than trying to feed it in after it is laid, it is also important when doing this not to have mortar on your hands as it will mark the facing edge of the brick, which will be unsightly. An easy and foolproof way to get a good bit of mortar on the end of the brick is to hold it over the wheelbarrow and effectively throw the mortar at the end of the brick (B). By holding the brick with the facing edges to the bottom they will not be affected by any misses and the excess can be cut off quickly with a trowel to give the shape shown. This brick can then be butted up against the existing wall to slightly squash the mortar in the joint and then checked for level, adjusting as necessary.

If the level of the brick needs adjusting because it is too high it can be knocked slightly on the end to squash it down into the bed of mortar. This is most easily achieved using the wooden end of a lump hammer (C) – do not be tempted to use the metal end as it will definitely split the brick. It is a good idea to avoid using the handle of the trowel as it will shower everything with the mortar left on the face of the trowel, although I must admit I frequently do use it none the less. If the brick is too low a bit more mortar needs to be added, in this case the best thing to do is not to simply add a little more but to take out what was under the brick, chuck it back in the wheelbarrow and lay the brick again. The reason for this is that as soon as the mortar is between the bricks they will suck all the water out of it, which is how the bond between brick and mortar is formed. If you then take the brick off again it will destroy this bond and make a very weak wall.

D

As already mentioned it is throughout essential to try and avoid getting mortar on the faces of the bricks because it will stain them. It is important therefore not to get mortar on your hands as this will get all over the bricks as well – it's not too good for the hands either as mortar is quite alkaline. In terms of finishing the wall off it is best to leave the bricks and mortar in an 'as laid' state for an hour or so and then go back and point the wall. This is done with the end of the trowel, pushing the mortar into the joints and striking off excess to give a slightly recessed shape to the joints. After an hour the bricks will have absorbed a lot of the water out of the mortar making it a lot more solid and easier to point.

It is often necessary to cut bricks, for example to form the half brick required at the start of every second course of a stretcher bond wall. In this case, where a half brick is required to form a header in the outer skin, it is usually best to cut the brick in half and lay it with the cut edge at the back of the wall. This leaves the neat factory produced corners on view.

In order to actually cut the bricks a bolster chisel is used. First mark the brick all round with the broad chisel before laying the brick on a flat surface and hitting it with enough force to split it. If the initial marking was sufficiently deep the brick will split along these lines, giving a nice square, clean cut. Bricks can have odd corners knocked off with the aid of a brickie's hammer – a hammer with a square head and an elongated, chisel-like tail instead of a claw or a ball. I find this an invaluable tool.

FLEMISH WALL BONDING

Flemish bond walling is built up in the same way using the same techniques, but both the side and end of some of the bricks need mortar applied before they are laid in – this takes a little practice but is not a difficult skill to acquire. Some bricks will also need to be trimmed down to make the 'queens closures' (half bricks longitudinally) at the beginning of every second course. These can be cut down with either a chisel or a brickie's hammer in older, soft bricks or with an angle grinder or disc saw with modern, more brittle bricks. The same applies to English bond walling.

BLOCK WALLING

As with bricks, there is some variation in the types of block available. The main variation is in the material the block is made of – the most useful types to the garden railway builder are thermalite blocks, which are the light four inch blocks often used in house construction, and concrete blocks, which are much heavier and available in four inch or six inch widths.

Thermalite blocks are ideally suited to forming the inner skin of a nine inch wall if bricks are used on the outside and blocks on the inside. They are light enough to be easy to lay but still sufficiently strong to easily support the weight of a railway on top. Concrete blocks are better suited to major civil engineering projects as they are much more solid, for example the construction of a retaining wall behind a new shed or similar. They can be laid either upright or on their sides. Six inch concrete blocks, it is worth noting, are fairly heavy – about 20kg each.

There are slight differences between laying blocks and bricks, as would be expected considering their very different sizes. It is more important to actually lay a flat bed of mortar (A) to sit the block on rather than the haphazard pyramid technique adopted with bricks. It is also more difficult to put the mortar on the end of the block before it is laid, and it can be easier, particularly when working in a trench, to feed the mortar in between the blocks (D). This is done with the aid of a bit of wood which is held against the back of the wall to stop the mortar falling out the back. The mortar is then dropped on top of the joint and fed in with the trowel, ramming it in well in order to form a good strong joint.

WOODEN SUPPORTING STRUCTURES

If brick or block walling is not to your taste, timber provides a very viable alternative supporting structure for a railway. It is cheaper and involves less work to put up, but is less durable and requires more long-term maintenance – a good coat of preservative every now and again and occasional spot replacement of failed component parts. In the case of a ground level or close to ground level line timber is a far easier material to use and there is no need for particularly heavy sections to take the load of a garden railway – two inch square posts can be used supporting either a plywood or sawn timber trackbase for lines anything up to a foot or so off the ground.

For these lower level timber sub bases a post is required every three feet or so and the track base can be attached directly to this. There is no need for anything more sophisticated. As the line gets further off the ground larger posts are required, which will need to be sunk further into the ground – three inch square posts are perfectly adequate for most applications. As the posts get more expensive it is cheaper overall to space them further apart and to install runners under the trackbase to allow it to span between the posts; this arrangement is shown below.

These posts can either be driven into the ground or placed in a hole and the soil backfilled around them – I would recommend the former approach for smaller posts and the latter for larger ones. If you are going to drive the posts into the ground make sure they have a point on the bottom to allow them easy passage into the ground – preferably a four sided one to stop them wandering away from the place you want them to go in. It isn't difficult to cut these on with the aid of a workmate and a decent saw or, if you buy two inch square survey pegs from a timber merchant, they will come pre-prepared with a point on the end. If you are putting these in you need them a good six to eight inches in the ground to get a solid trackbase – you can generally feel when it's getting solid enough to build a railway on. With larger posts it is easier to dig a hole, place the post in it and backfill around it either with concrete or ballast rammed hard in the hole. The latter is good as it allows some drainage away from the post preventing it rotting so quickly and, as a material, can be rammed well in but without the permanence and expense of concrete. A handy way of buying three inch square timber is to buy fence posts and cut them in half or thirds – this often works out cheapest.

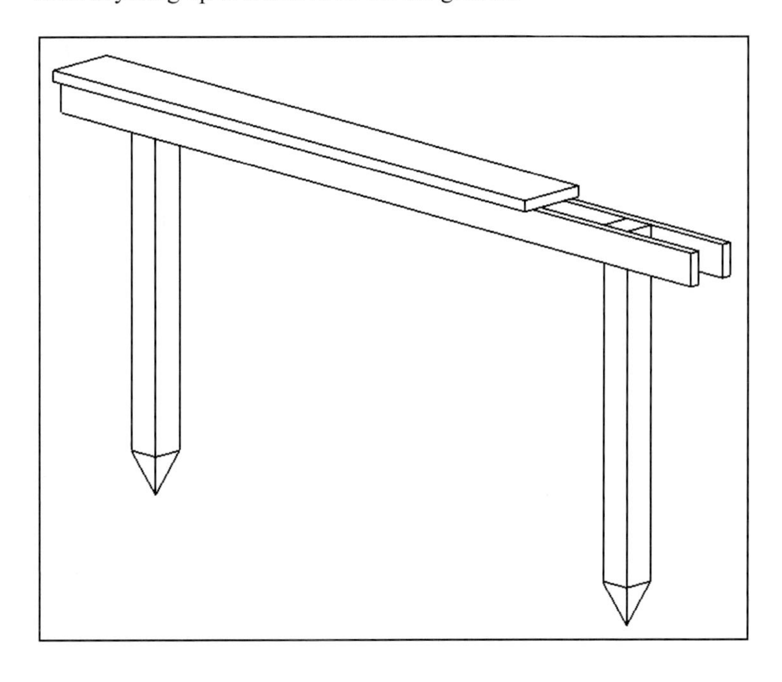

Arrangement for wooden supporting structure for a trackbase higher than 18" or so off the ground with larger posts further apart for economy and runners under the trackbase to span between the posts.

4

THE MAJOR CIVIL ENGINEERING WORK

Whereas the infrastructure which is such a part of the prototype railway scene tends to be purely aesthetic for inside railways, with tunnels conveniently located at the end of stations to lead off the fiddle yard and bridges built but seldom, in the garden they are as important a part of the railway route as on the real thing, spanning ponds or the corners of patios or diving under the garden path. The garden railway builder needs to approach bridge and tunnel construction in a completely different manner to his indoor counterpart, building bridges which support the trains in the same way as the prototype rather than the cosmetic exercises frequently employed inside. The same is true of tunnels, which actually have to carry the line under paths, steps or the rockery rather than just through the backscene into the fiddle yard behind.

Bridges are an area of railway modelling which I feel are often misunderstood, and, as with designing layouts, I would urge that, if in doubt, follow the prototype. I have been equally amused and distressed by some bridges I have seen modelled over the years which just look completely wrong, and can ruin a view of a layout which could otherwise look so realistic. As bridges in the garden tend to have to physically span between abutments they have to work in the same way as the real thing. They often are on a completely different scale to bridges inside, too – you may need a tall viaduct taking the track across a low section of the garden, and a bridge carrying the line of metals across the pond could well be required to be several feet long. In order to build these bridges realistically and durably it is necessary to understand them, and I hope that

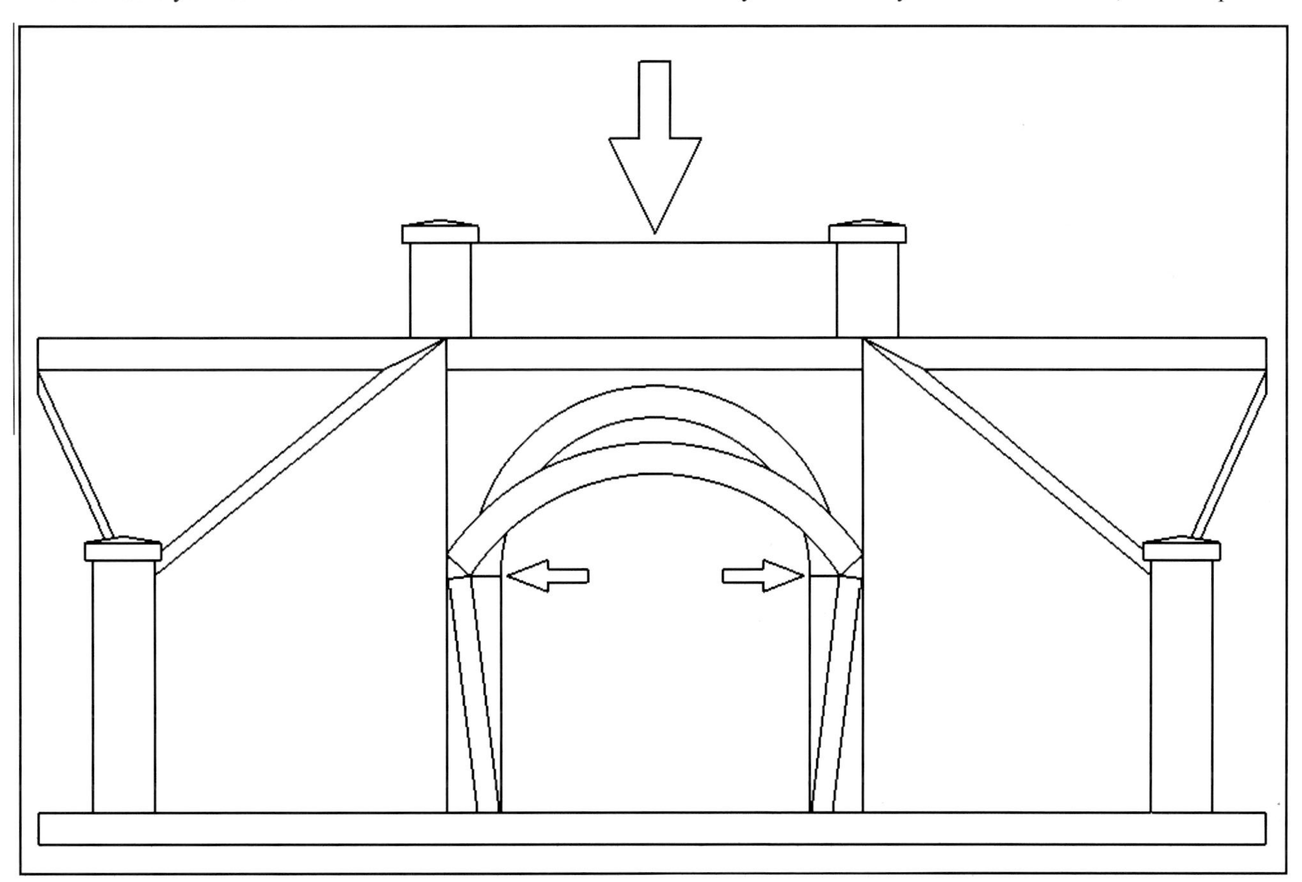

How an arch bridge or tunnel works. The load (the big arrow) is carried by misshaping the arch (ever so slightly), thus forcing it to take on the bowed shape shown at the bottom. It is by doing this that the ends of the arch which are restrained by the abutments and the earth on either side are forced outwards – and it is by this restraint that the bridge is physically held up. The actual deformation is incredibly small if there is any at all, but the way that a bridge would collapse is a sure indication of how the load is carried.

you will forgive the little bit of theory below which I have included to explain what should happen to allow bridges to support a load, and thus enable you to build bridges which will span with grace and ease across a gap into which some of the bridges I have seen over the years would simply fold up and tumble.

BRIDGES

There are a huge number of railway bridges in the United Kingdom. There must be very few miles of track which don't cross a culvert, pass under a road or arch over a viaduct and yet they are relatively infrequently modelled - mainly, I would imagine, because when building a model railway inside, the landscape that the railway passes through can be deliberately created to minimise the number of bridges required, and in doing this culverts and small over bridges are often engineered out of existence. In the garden, however, the landscape already exists, and bridges are far more likely to be needed.

THE MECHANICS OF REAL BRIDGES

There are two basic types of bridging mechanism commonly used on the railways – the arch and the beam. Trusses – often frequently used - are simply a beam with bits of the web cut out to save steel. Arches are the simplest to understand, and their technology can be traced back to the Romans who understood just what a good way of spanning across gaps they are.

As the load is applied on the top of the bridge it travels down through the fill to the actual arch itself, built usually of either stone, brick or concrete. In trying to squash the top of the arch downwards the load applied would change the shape of the arch slightly, were it able to, pushing it outwards at the ends - an effect which can be observed by bending a postcard into an arch shape and pushing the top down slightly. This change in shape of the arch, shown by the small horizontal arrows in the diagram below, mirrors the transfer of force through the arch structure - and the manner in which the arch would deflect, were it allowed, accurately portrays the way it supports the load.

In reality the tops of the abutments at the end of the arch do not move outwards, but are restrained by the fill behind - the embankment, in the case of an overbridge, or the cutting side for an underbridge. It is by resisting this movement that the bridge carries the load of a railway or road or footpath imposed upon it. The abutments of an arch bridge are therefore critical, and cannot be simply ignored as occasionally seen on model railways. They take the actual load of the bridge, and there have been some spectacular collapses over the years when they have failed.

Tunnels work in exactly the same way, being basically extended arch bridges supported by the sides of the hill all around; therefore they cannot be built too close to the edge of a cliff in soft ground because there would be no support on one side of the arch, quickly leading to a similarly spectacular failure.

Beam bridges are slightly more complicated and generally used in different locations. Whereas arch bridges are usually found in short-span locations, beams are generally used to span longer distances. If we imagine a steel 'I' beam spanning between two supports, the load on the middle of the beam makes the beam sag through its weight. As the beam sags it changes shape, and forces in the top and bottom flanges result. It is through the beam resisting these forces that the load is supported. As the beam takes on a slightly curved shape the bottom of the beam goes into tension as the new curved shape of the beam requires it to get a bit longer. The top goes into compression because it is trying to get shorter as a result of becoming curved. This means that through the middle of the beam you get a 'neutral axis', which is where there is no force at all as the tension on one side and compression on the other effectively cancel each other out. This is why holes drilled into a beam - for example to support a pipe hitching a lift across a cutting supported by a beam of a bridge - are generally drilled in the middle of the beam to avoid removing material where it is actually carrying load at the edges of the beam.

By putting the top of the beam in compression you are essentially trying to squash the metal up there, and as a result of this there is quite a force outwards where the metal is trying to buckle out to one side or the other to avoid having to get shorter. To restrain this it is usual to rivet or weld some stiffeners onto the web of the beam (the

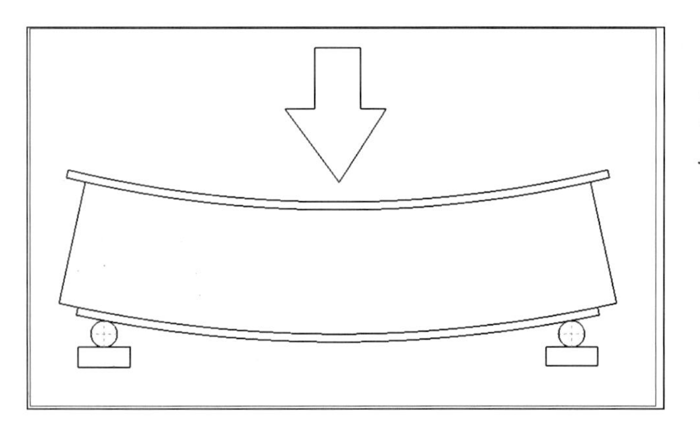

How a beam bridge deforms under load, indicating how it carries the force of a train running over it and how the top flange goes into compression and the bottom into tension.

Meldon Viaduct on the old LSWR route round the back of Dartmoor. There's masses of detail here to interest the modeller, but most importantly notice the difference between the diagonal ties running in opposite directions – those at the far end of the span are just two flat strips sloping away from the camera as these are resisting tension, whereas their counterparts sloping towards the camera are braced to resist compression. The tension ties nearest the camera are different again, with some additional stiffening to resist the bigger moment in the middle of the span. There are actually two separate viaducts here, the original behind the more modern steel one. It must have seemed awfully tall and spindly up there, back when it was a single track viaduct on a blustery winter's night with the Dartmoor rain blowing horizontally into the cab...

plate separating the top and bottom flanges); these are the plates which make railway bridges so instantly recognisable. This effect is also the reason why, virtually without exception, beams in bridges are always straight in plan – if you start curving the beam you are just making it far too tempting for the compression flange to buckle out on the curve. Curved steel railway bridges are actually almost always a collection of shorter straight railway bridges over which the tracks are laid on a curve.

The actual amount of load the bridge can support is directly related to the distance the top and bottom flanges are spaced apart, or the depth of the beam – deeper beams, with every other dimension the same, support more load. There is a relationship, therefore, between the span and depth of a beam – this is usually in the order of 20:1.

As an extension of trying to position the flanges further and further apart (enabling smaller section flanges to be used, which in the long run is cheaper) trusses were developed. These take the well-known form shown in the figure above. A truss is really just a beam with the web in the middle cut out, as it is simply not needed. It is replaced instead by diagonal braces which carry alternately tension and compression between the two flanges, which is why adjacent ties in the middle of a truss are often different with two types employed in a bridge – one carrying tension and one compression. This arrangement is clearly visible in the view of Meldon viaduct in Devon.

While the decks of bridges are relatively advanced mechanisms carrying the load the piers are dead simple, usually carrying pure compression loading. All the

A bridge which has actually failed, demonstrating, in the process, that the tension flange along the bottom of the bridge is essential and not to be forgotten! The web has cracked beside the fourth stiffener from the left as it was simply unable to withstand the pulling force along the bottom of the bridge. This happened as I was cleaning the track in the middle of an operating session, due doubtless to the law of a certain Irishman, and I was able to mend it temporarily by bending a bit of brass strip up to pull the third and fifth stiffeners towards each other. Far better however would have been to have just built the bridge right in the first place.

It is this kind of structure that offers a real challenge to the garden railway builder, and to be honest straddles the boundary of what I could realistically advocate trying to construct outside. Never one to resist a challenge however, I'm sure the deed could be done...

Not only, as would be the case for an inside layout, is the construction of the trestles likely to be tricky to say the least - particularly with those fancy handrails (there were some prototypes with much simpler handrails than that shown here) – but in the garden the structure must be weatherproof too. It would be nearly impossible to model a structure such as this in a totally weatherproof fashion, short of building the entire thing from brass section with soldered joints. While this would make a very rigid and virtually indestructible viaduct, it is considerably beyond the limit of most people's wallets. It is instead necessary to adopt a degree of compromise, and decide how much maintenance the engineer is prepared to carry out, and how much he is prepared to spend at the outset to avoid this becoming necessary.

There is no perfect material for building something such as this in the garden. The real things were, of course, built from wood to limit capital expenditure, and construction from wooden sections also represents the cheapest solution in model form. Only dense, fine-grained hardwood however would last the winter spent outside, and softwood and balsa wood would stand no chance. The problem with modelling bridges such as this from timber is that, in model form, it degrades at the same rate as on the real thing – however there is considerably less depth to the sections to start with. Whereas a little surface degradation perhaps a quarter of an inch deep on the 18 inch square baulks of Brunel's structures was neither here nor there, in model form, the entire piece of timber is likely only to be quarter of an inch square and would be rendered entirely useless by such an attack.

Large plasticard sections are slightly more resilient to the weather and won't rot in any way, although plasticard can go brittle over time if constantly exposed to UV light. More of a problem is that connecting plastic together is difficult in a weatherproof manner as most solvent glued joints become very brittle over time. Evostick tends to work a bit better than a true solvent glue, producing a slightly flexible, marginally more ductile joint - however even these joints, I find, occasionally dry out and come apart over time.

Faced with the challenge of constructing one of these viaducts, I think I would adopt a hybrid approach – brass section for the main uprights and cross beams on the outside fans (dotted in the drawing) and possibly aluminium strip bolted to the top of this structure to support the track (shown hatched), the whole sat atop concrete piers, which would form a rigid bridge. The rest of the viaduct – the central fans and other bracing – could then be built from plasticard, attached to the brass with a contact adhesive and well painted against degradation from the sun.

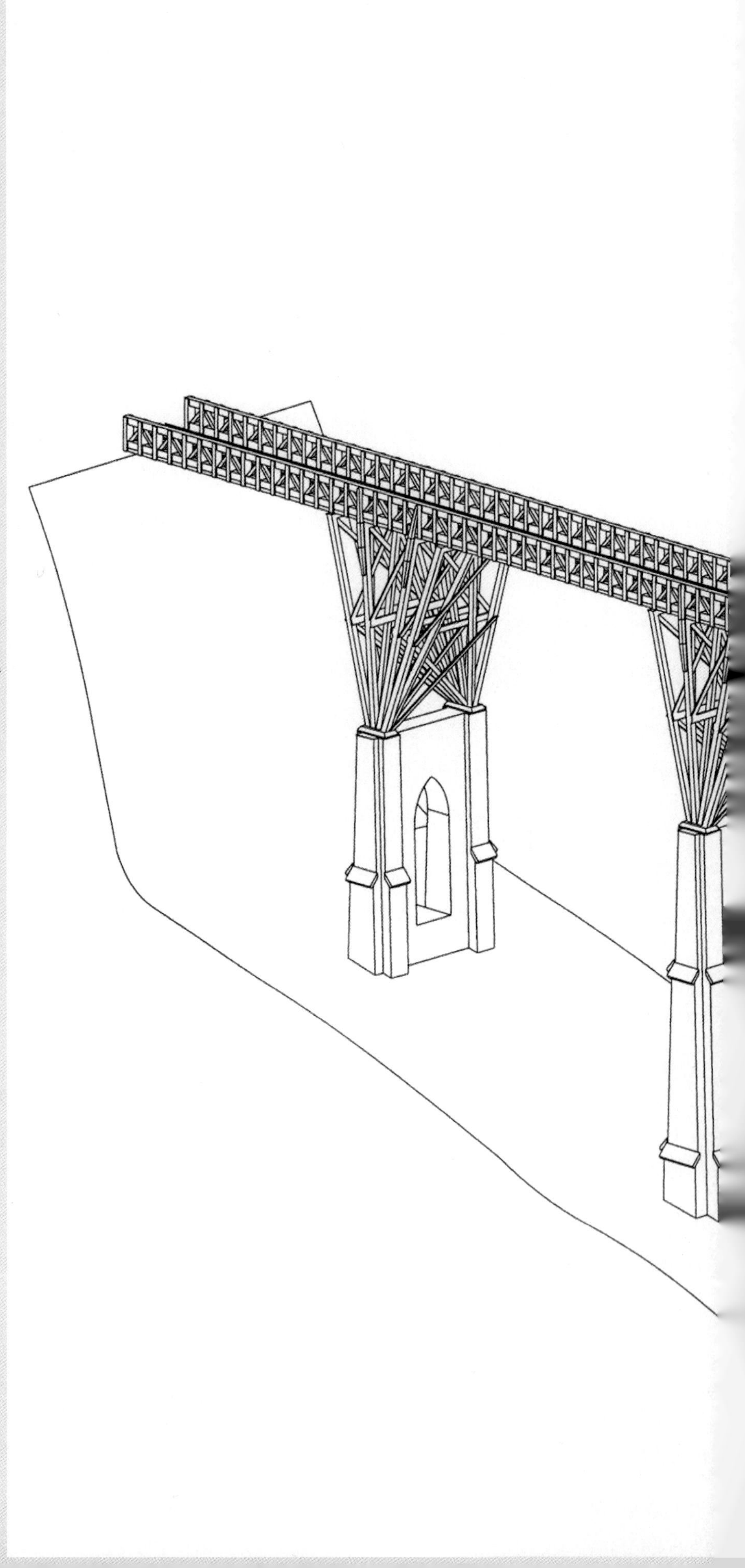

engineer has to do is make them big enough and of a suitably strong material not to squash under the load.

BUILDING BRIDGES IN THE GARDEN

The way in which the construction of a bridge for a garden railway should proceed depends on the type of bridge itself. Arch bridges more or less have to be cast out of concrete, whereas beam bridges can be built up in a number of different ways. These two are dealt with separately below.

ARCH BRIDGES

Because of their shape by far the easiest way to build arch bridges is to cast them in a mould. This is true of both single span overbridges and multi span viaducts – in fact it is easiest to build viaducts out of lots of concrete units cast out of the same mould. The mould I constructed to cast the four arch viaduct on my line in was built out of plywood with sections of guttering used to form the underside of the arch. Only the top was cast, down to just below the top of the piers – the rest of the piers were built up from cement using the mix of 3:1:1 (sharp sand : building sand : cement) I use as standard for virtually all things railway related. The arches can be cast in either fine concrete or the same sand and cement mix – I used concrete with some ten millimetre aggregate in it, but I wouldn't recommend using anything bigger than this in the way of aggregate as, if it ends up in the face of the viaduct, it will look a bit odd. The mould needs to be built constantly bearing in mind that it will need to come apart again to get the arch out, to which end I would recommend screwing it all together rather than nailing. It's worth leaving it for a few days – three should be fine – before taking it apart, particularly leaving it well alone for the first 12 hours' curing or so, and keep it damp - or at least not outside in direct sunlight – which will make the concrete stronger in the long run.

It can be worth putting some chicken wire or bent coat hangers over the tops of the arches, not so much to act as conventional reinforcement but rather as a crack control measure; should a crack develop the reinforcement will keep the arch together and prevent the viaduct falling apart. I left some rawl plugs in the top of the arches as I cast them with the intention that I would put in some screws to act as a key for the parapets when I built them – although I have yet to do this five years on, as I suspect that were I to put a screw in it would break the concrete. Better would have been to have drilled the rawl plugs in after casting in the more conventional manner, or to have pushed some nails in to the top of the concrete along the edge when it was wet to provide a key for the sidewalls. The parapets will (one day) be built up just like a wall as explained in the 'buildings' section which follows.

BEAM BRIDGES

Beam bridges, in which category I include trusses, can be built up out of a large range of materials. Plasticard (styrene sheet) is probably easiest, and certainly my favourite medium, but aluminium or wood are possibilities. I have a couple of wooden viaducts which are removable and cross the path to the shed on my line. Wood is the perfect material for this kind of location where a bit of two by one on edge will span for miles, but they don't look terribly realistic, and the smaller sections which would be required to build realistic looking bridges would quickly rot, I fear. For spans around the foot mark I usually use 40 thou plasticard and Evostick for solidarity, building up the 'I' beams out of lots of strips as shown in figure overleaf. For my 'OO' gauge line it is easy to place the main beams right next to each other under the rails to form a compact but very, very strong little box section – the bridge over the pond supported several bricks before I lost my nerve piling them on, envisaging a fairly spectacular failure.

Wherever a butt joint between two sections of plastic is required when building up a bridge structure I reinforce it with copious amounts of 100 thou square strip – bridges are one thing it is absolutely worth building solidly, as it is most annoying having to come back and rebuild them later if they have fallen apart.
Walkways are added down either side of the bridge, again in plasticard, handrails from scrap rail and brass wire complete the job.

Smaller bridges can be easily built up out of the pre-formed 'I' beam sections available on the modelling market, as is the little occupation crossing bridge in the figure overleaf. A couple of cross braces keep the two sides together, and again the whole makes a very strong little bridge. For spans of this length the track will actually span quite happily on its own and support the weight of a passing train, but something of a bridge under the rails tends to make other people a whole lot happier when they're thinking of running their stock on your line.

I had a lot of trouble for a while with that much mentioned but most annoying problem of the ground moving separately at either end of the old bridge across the pond. I got a little irritated, I must confess, by the alignment never staying where I put it across the bridge, and during its reconstruction I put in great long supports of three by two inch timber as the main abutments – while these are undoubtedly on the large side, they weren't hard to knock in with a sledgehammer and will definitely never move. The central pier just rests on the bottom of the pond – I'm fairly certain had I cut it through the liner it never would have sealed and a concrete block under the liner and the rest of the pier on top forms a more than adequate foundation. The two extremities of the bridge are still free to move in and out, being bolted down only in the middle, and restrained side to side at the ends to allow for any small movement which may occur without unduly stressing the bridge. The track over the bridge is glued to it

A small span beam bridge in the garden, almost akin to an occupation crossing. Two plastistrut 'I' beam sections have been glued together so the webs are directly under the rails, and these were then supported on mortar bearing pads which keep them up tight under the rails. This makes a very strong bridge indeed, especially over short lengths such as this.

with Evostick to maintain some semblance of a decent alignment.

Bridges are, of course, another area of garden railway building where there is so much variation in the solutions which could be employed that it is impossible to cover all the options here. As so often stated in these pages, if in doubt, refer to the prototype!

Occasionally of course, things like paths just get in the way of the railway, and a more functional bridge is required. Wood makes the perfect building material for what is likely to be a bridge stored out of the weather when not in use. A piece of three by one will span a good couple of feet with a person stood on it, and if you add a bit of two by one on edge under it you can span, as I mentioned earlier, for pretty large distances. A bridge spanning the path to the shed is shown overleaf. The ends are oak with brass dowels let in to locate the track and ensure a well aligned joint.

TUNNELS

Tunnels are a lot simpler to build than bridges, in my opinion. Rather than the long and difficult bored tunnels of the real railways we are only really interested in building relatively short cut and cover tunnels – under a rockery or a path. When planning these it is important to remember that access needs to be possible along the entire length of the tunnel to clean the track, flush out the cobwebs and rescue derailed stock. While it is tempting to believe that most of these functions could be carried out at the end of a pole I would recommend against it, making sure it is actually possible to access the entire tunnel by hand. Access ports can be built in the middle of course, a purpose built cover or conventional manhole being used to

A quick 'load test' of a beam bridge built up from plasticard before installation in the garden. Bridges like this will easily support the heaviest of trains – several bricks and you might start worrying. The main beams are those directly under the rails, on which the track is laid directly, just visible in the span in the foreground. The stiffeners on the web of the far span double as the supports for the footways down either side of the bridge.

Building up the walling around the central pier of the bridge. The 'capstone' has also been installed in this view, as have the holding down bolts – only the centre of the bridge is held fixed in position, while the ends are free to slide. It is important that the wood is wet when you surround it in cement as, if not, it will absorb water when you fill the pond, promptly expand and crack the cement around the outside of the post that you have just spent so long building up. I haven't applied any preservative as I can't imagine it being very pond-life friendly, so I am instead relying on the principle that timber which is always wet won't rot. Time will tell if this is a valid assumption... If it proves not, I'm confident that the cement surround around the pier will take the load of the bridge – garden railways really don't impose a very heavy loading on the structures supporting them.

cover the hole. I find a couple of feet the longest length of tunnel that allows easy access right the way through.

Tunnel construction takes two basic forms – either using wood or bricks and concrete. I have only ever used wood to build tunnels, which is much easier, but I have to admit less durable. I took a tunnel out once and the back of the three quarter inch ply had actually rotted worryingly significantly where it had been in contact with the ground all the time. Beyond ease of construction, the chief advantage of wood is that it is a bit more forgiving when you graze your knuckles on it cleaning the track. There is nothing difficult to a wooden tunnel – it's just a box in the ground designed to the dimensions of the biggest bit of rolling stock, making sure you can also get your hand through.

Brick tunnels are the Rolls Royce of the business, guaranteed to live through most things you can throw at them. A two course wall down either side of the track base will give the right kind of height, and the roof can either be a brick spanning crossways or a paving slab or similar – these will happily span the six inches or so tunnels tend to be wide. It is important to use engineering bricks, or at the very least partial engineering bricks, as normal bricks will not last underground, absorbing far too much water. Old reclaimed bricks would probably be fine as, despite absorbing large quantities of water, they aren't affected by it anything like as badly as modern bricks - but then burying these more expensive and better-looking bricks does seems a bit of a waste somehow.

The completed bridge in action as a very old Lima flying banana gets the revs on to tackle the gradient up to Grogley Junction.

A functional bridge spanning the garden path, in this case simply a length of three by one. The oak arrangement at the end can be made out – this is to give a good positive location for the dowels and screws holding the rails in place, more so than you could achieve with the softwood

The trackbase itself can either be concrete or wood screwed to the concrete foundation - personally I would favour the latter to have something completely flat to nail the track to and to keep it in alignment.

The floor of the tunnel needs to be on a slight gradient to get the water to run out – if the track is level through the tunnel the base can slope up either side of a summit in the middle or the concrete base slope under a level wooden trackbed – in either case the slope need only be extremely slight, 1:100 or so, and in short tunnels hardly noticeable. It is important not to dismiss it for this reason though as the trackbase and, if it is built out of wood, the tunnel will rot very quickly if water collects in it.

Tunnel portals are needed at either end to hide the actual construction of the tunnel and make them look realistic. The same plastic ones as used inside can be pressed into service, or concrete ones cast in situ - or for the narrow gauge modeller, they can be built up from slate or similar to give the impression of a tunnel hewn from the rock face. Casting tunnel mouths in situ is fairly straightforward – I tend to use a few sheets of card from cornflakes packets as centring to cast it against, which works surprisingly well. The standard 3:1:1 mix is knocked up and then placed relatively carefully over three thicknesses of roughly three inch wide strips of card, building up either side at the same time. It pushes out of shape a bit at this stage, but once you get the crown loaded the card acts as a true arch, and you can alter the cement to take the correct shape before it starts to dry, during which process the card supports it. After it is dry the card can be removed and you have a free standing tunnel portal ready for the trains. This works well for single track locations, although I suspect in scales bigger than 'O' gauge, this method of construction probably wouldn't have the strength to support itself, and a more conventional formwork supported on wood would be required. The surface can be scribed when partially dry for stonework, but this always looks over scale to my eye – by building up the sharp sand mix by hand the resulting rough finish looks significantly more realistic, especially from a slight distance.

The wooden superstructure of an unfinished tunnel and with a half finished coach to check the loading gauge. Of course, once I had built the whole thing and cast the portals in place I realised this isn't actually the biggest coach I have at all... I recommend getting this right, as trying to explain that my four wheel brake with large duckets is route restricted is like an invitation for people to run it down and see if it'll fit through the tunnel!

CUTTINGS AND EMBANKMENTS

As much a part of the real railway as rails and sleepers are cuttings and embankments, and these have been modelled on inside layouts for years in the familiar mess of plaster, scrim and chicken wire. Earthworks such as these are possibly the only thing that I would actually warn against outside and admit to being more difficult to get working outside than in. The problem is that whereas inside earth banks are pure representations, from completely different materials, outside they are actually earth, which is where all the problems start.

Earth doesn't scale between the real thing and the model, and whereas the slope of a cutting on the real thing is probably accurate to a foot or two, you're trying to achieve an accuracy of a few millimetres with a model with exactly the same material. And the problems don't stop there. On a garden railway you will almost definitely be constructing earthworks with topsoil whereas on the prototype they would chuck that a long way away and just use good solid subsoil, which would look absolutely hideous in the garden, being something like pure clay or solid chalk. Topsoil just moves as soon as it rains – it doesn't really compact and it ends up getting either washed out from under the trackbase in the case of an embankment or washed down onto the track in the case of a cutting, meaning you actually have to dig the track out after a winter.

If you are going to build cuttings, and sometimes they're unavoidable, I would recommend lining them with something other than soil. You could use mortar and effectively shotcrete the cutting walls, but this does make a bit of an abrasive surface which may scratch the paintwork off the sides of your nice trains if you have a derailment. I have made quite extensive use of slate to edge cuttings, which I find works quite well - a big lump from a garden centre can often be split down to a vast number of little bits, which can be cemented in place. While not an ideal solution as it leaves fairly unprototypical joints between the separate bits of slate, it works a lot better than digging the track out of the mud every spring.

Embankments I would just avoid, even planting them with some low ground-cover type plant doesn't really protect them - as eventually all the soil ends up at the bottom and you can see right under the trackbase. I just build walls up either side of the trackbase – there are few prototypical examples, I would have to grant you, but there are some – the vast slate embankments of the Ffestiniog spring to mind. I build these walls up using the methods explained in the 'building the built environment' section.

The beginning of the arch casting process. A couple of layers of card at least are required as the top one goes soggy, the print preventing the water penetrating to the second layer. In this picture the two dollops of mortar on either side are just holding the arch in place, the next stage is to build the mortar up and over the top, which should be possible all in one go, such is the strength of the arch shape. The important thing is to keep the level of the mortar on the two sides of the arch equal – if you don't it will push the arch out of shape and eventually collapse it. Normally I carry mortar around the garden on a board, but if that is too big to put down conveniently close to the workplace, as here, an empty sand bag is a useful alternative.

The whole portal can be cast in one go as below, although my nerve failed when it came to needing to press the headwall together a bit to get rid of those cracks at the top. The headwall as built as a conventional wall the following day.

5

LAYING THE TRACK

The track itself takes on a particular importance in a garden railway. Not only is there a lot more of it, therefore increasing the potential for faults, but derailments also tend to be a lot more frustrating, seeming always to be in the most inaccessible of places, and under the most spiky of bushes. In order to realise the full potential of a garden railway, enjoying hours of successful operation and being able to leave it to run on its own while sitting back to enjoy the spectacle from afar, particular care needs to be exercised when laying the track.

BUILDING THE TRACKBASE AND BALLASTING THE FORMATION

As mentioned in passing in the sections above, I strongly advocate the use of a wooden trackbase under the track. If the line is built on a brick wall it will even out any imperfections in this, and it will allow the alignment of the track to be carefully controlled and held rigidly in place. If the line is built on a wooden supporting structure then the track base will already be in place – in the case of a line on a wall, it will need to be installed. The same thick ply or sawn sectional timber can be used, screwed down on top of the wall. Personally I prefer to use ply for the bulk of the trackbase, especially for junctions and curves, although for long straights I tend to use three by one for convenience. I used to make extensive use of wood recovered from pallets for the trackbases on the line, but have moved away from this now – it does not come in sufficiently long lengths to make it worthwhile for straight sections, and I recommend avoiding using short lengths of straight trackbase to get round curves or lots of thin boards next to each other for junction locations. You end up going round curves or across junctions on lots of different bits of wood all at

A piece of ply cut for a specific location. In this case both the end of the station and the curve benefit from being on one large sheet of ply, and by making the bits of trackbase as big as possible like this the best possible alignment and running are ensured. It is worth considering at this stage things like point motors and so on, which will all eventually need mounting – in this case a piece of ply is provided adjacent to the turnout on the splice on the left.

slightly different angles, which makes achieving a decent alignment, particularly vertically, difficult and often results in lots of twists. The trains will run significantly better in these instances if the track is supported on just one large piece of ply cut specifically for the location.

Once cut to the appropriate shape and given a coat of preservative, I attach the trackbase to the sub-base with a rawl plug every couple of feet, which forms a perfectly adequate connection. If the top of the wall is a bit uneven the slack can be taken up with a few scraps of roofing felt to get the top level – it is essential that there are no sudden changes of height or cross level between sections of track base.

I recommend using a strip of roofing felt under the track to give the impression of ballast and to ease out any slight imperfections which may remain to ensure a good alignment to the track. The cheapest felt can be used in fact, - that designed for sheds often sold as 'mineralised' roofing felt is best as it is finished with a layer of fine chippings which give the impression of ballast. To mark the track use an old piece of track and a nail. You want a good long bit of flexitrack which has been outside for a while as the oxidisation of the rail will mean it sticks in the clips on the sleepers, so when you bend it the track will

Drilling through the trackbase and into the bricks beneath with a masonry bit for the rawl plugs.

Marking out ballast with an old piece of track and a nail.

retain its shape. You can therefore just bend the track to the required radius on the trackbase, move it carefully across to the roll of felt and mark the shape out with the aid of an old nail or similar, which leaves a white mark on the felt. This can then be cut out with an old pair of scissors – under no circumstances use new scissors, the felt will ruin them. If the felt has got creased by being stored rolled up and the roll then squashed, laying it out in the sun will quickly flatten it out again.

In the case of junctions it is often necessary to mark out slightly more complicated shapes. In my experience, drawing a line down the middle of the junction and then measuring along it and taking offsets to critical points to measure out the shape of the ballast is often the easiest way to mark out any complicated shapes required. You can always over-judge it a bit and then trim it back in situ.

Once you have completed this stage you will have a nice new section of formation with a neat line of ballast stretching off to the next station, wanting only for a line of metals before the trains can actually get running.

An example of how not to do it! Even outside, it is worth getting things like the 'six foot' – the distance between adjacent tracks – right. This layout annoyed me so much I rebuilt it the year after this picture was taken, squeezing the tracks together to a more prototypical distance. I also had the diamond for the double junction in the foreground rebuilt to get a considerably better alignment through here – a case of it being worth building a bit of track in a fairly unusual situation where proprietary track just wouldn't fit. Although it might at first look okay in this photo it rapidly became a single line under the plant on the left, and the connection onto this single line was a truly dreadful case of being a series of corners as opposed to a curve.

TYPES OF TRACK

Most garden railways I know are laid with proprietary track because the quantities involved far outstrip that which anyone would realistically want to build. My own modest 0-16.5 line in a small garden now has over 72 yards of plain line, and to have built this from scratch when PECO and similar products are available would have been very tedious. I also use a lot of proprietary S&C (switches and crossings – points, diamond crossings and the like). The space available in the garden means it is usually possible to design layouts around the geometric restrictions imposed by using standard units, and the techniques the manufacturers employ make them so accurate they virtually guarantee good running as long as they are well laid. There will always be situations where the geometry of the layout cannot be met by commercially available items, and in this case I use PCB construction to build the necessary bits of S&C. The details of this are well explained in other books, suffice for me to say that if made with reasonable PCB strip for the sleepers this type of track can quite happily survive outside for a long time. PECO track is perfectly suitable for outside use if it is laid as they recommend - out of constant direct sunlight - and if the springs in the turnouts are kept lubricated with electrolube. If the latter step is skipped they will, being steel, rust and eventually break.

Actually laying the track is a simple process - there is no difference really to laying track inside. I find 25mm verneer pins (smaller than panel pins) best for 0-16.5 track and just about okay with OO track, however smaller track than this and a smaller size would be required. Steel pins are perfectly adequate, and as the head rusts it turns a fairly un-noticeable colour whereas brass pins will always remain obvious and detract from the realism of the track, and I have never had a problem with the pins rusting through. The main benefit of using long pins to hold the track down is that they can be knocked in through the sleeper and just into the ballast but easily pulled out again for adjustment of the alignment, meaning the layout can easily be tweaked to perfection. When this stage has been finalised they can be knocked all the way in. Try to avoid hitting the rails with the hammer as this kinks them badly. Personally I have never had any real problem with expansion and contraction of the rails due to heat and I think this problem is frequently blown out of proportion by modellers considering a garden railway - a significantly greater threat is posed by the movement of the trackbase due to seasonal movements in the soil.

Gluing the track down is not very practical outside as the types of glues used to do this inside, PVA and the like - are not waterproof and therefore not suitable. The only alternatives - contact adhesives etc - are prohibitively expensive. Loose stone ballast can be used; however I would not recommend it unless you are prepared to really maintain it, frequently tamping it in under the track. For small scale lines (less than 'O' gauge or so) it is really not recommended because the smallest stone available is about three millimetre grade and far too big to form a good interlocking mass around smaller scale track to give it the necessary support. Some people have used small pegs driven into the ground to hold the track in alignment, however this tends to result in a very bad vertical alignment with high spots over the posts and low bits in between unless the ballast is maintained constantly and well tamped under the track.

It is very important and far more difficult to get the track laid well in the garden, partly because there is simply a lot more of it than generally found inside and partly because the base is generally slightly less perfectly level than inside. If the track is to run well it is essential to check both the line and the level of it - the railway terms used to describe the horizontal and vertical alignment of the track respectively. The only practical way to assess this is from track level, and well laid track is a sign of hours spent by the person who laid it down on their hands and knees at track level While this is, without doubt, not the most comfortable of positions there is a lot which can be done to improve the situation. Investing in a garden kneeler will save the knees, as will raising the track bed slightly - a single course wall or similar will reduce the amount of bending down required by a surprising amount. Many people are reluctant to get down on their hands and knees to lay track which I can quite understand, but it does make a real difference to the track and faults which are not at all visible whilst standing up are immediately very visible from a rail-level viewpoint.

Personally I try not to pin down S & C components unless absolutely unavoidable. There is a lot of potential, as you put the pins in, for hitting something you don't want to such as the switches or a check rail. If the plain line leading to the components is held down well there should be no force on the switch and crossing trying to move it out of alignment, and therefore it should stay where you want it. By 'held down well' I do not necessarily mean by lots of pins - three pins is sufficient to hold any curve in position with no outward force at the ends. In fact I would recommend trying to reduce the number of pins used as they affect the vertical alignment of the track considerably. I would also recommend moving, as far as practically possible, all kinds of joints off curves and onto straight sections of track, particularly block joints - the insulated fishplates have less rigidity than their nickel silver counterparts and tend to make creating a nice smooth curve very, very difficult. In the case of plain joints on a curved section of track I often solder the joints solid to ensure the curve carries on nicely through the joint and does not become a series of corners. If a joint on a curve is unavoidable, using pre-curved rails such as Peco Setrack on either side of an IBJ (Insulated Block Joint) will minimise the outwards force on the joint, improving the alignment through it. If the Setrack is to the wrong radius the rails can still be used, slid into some sleepers culled from a length of Flexitrack, and the resulting semi-flexi-track then being eased to the correct radius. While this sounds a slightly complicated procedure, in reality it's not that hard to achieve, and it does result in a nice smooth curve.

The advantage of the track – level viewpoint is evident from this view. Notice the bent-up rail joint just in front of the 08 – this is hardly visibly when standing. Information from this viewpoint is of huge value when trying to tweak the track a bit to get it to run better after a bad winter has twisted walls and trackbases slightly out of alignment.

COMMON TRACK FAULTS

Track faults and the reasons why trains derail are another area of railway modelling which I feel is often misunderstood. This section demonstrates some of the common faults found and explains some ways to rectify them. Track faults are potentially a more significant problem for garden railway builders than for their inside-based counterparts for a number of reasons, not least of which the fact that garden railways have to cope with the weather, and the sheer volume of track on the average garden layout is a lot greater than that which most people use inside.

FAULTS IN THE LINE OF THE TRACK

Curves have a habit of being the place where most derailments occur because of the way the wheels travel round them. On a piece of straight track the wheels tend to sit between the rails running on the wheel tread - the slightly inclined bit of the wheel roughly parallel to the axle – so neither flange is in direct contact with the rail head. This means that slight fluctuations in the alignment on a straight, particularly at the joints, do not have a disastrous effect on the trains. On a curve however the flange on the outside of the curve will be pressed hard

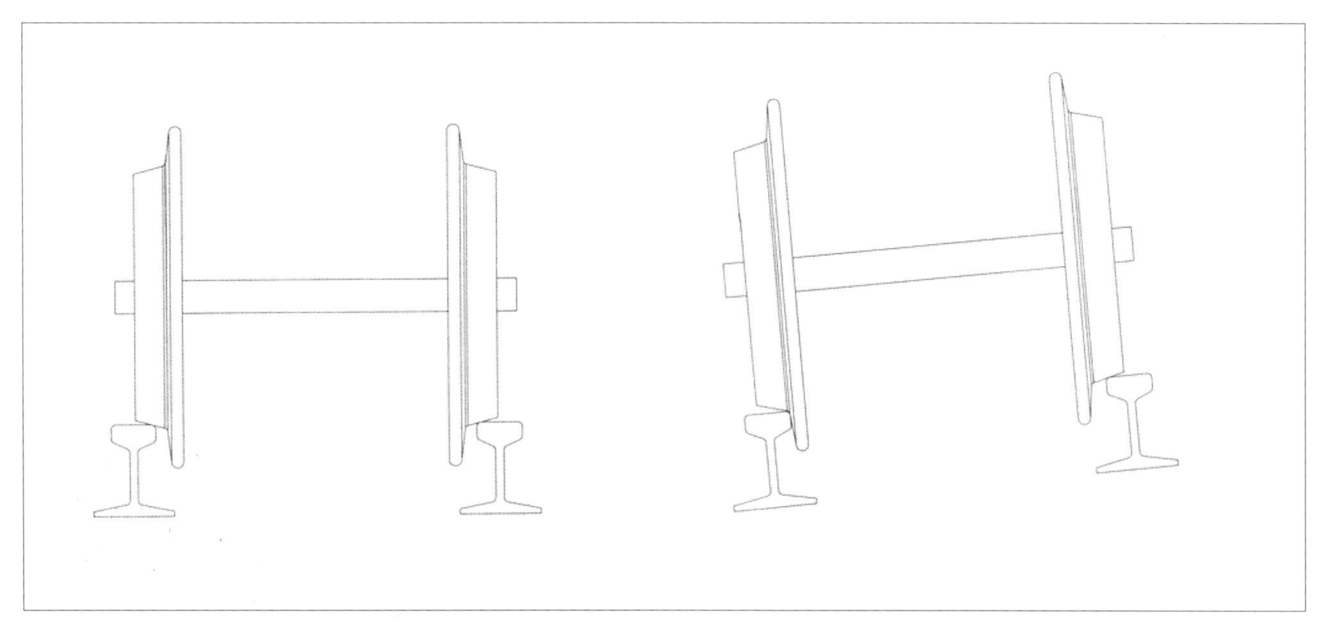

Wheels running on straight (left) and curved (right) track. Notice how on the straight neither flange is pressed against the rail edge, whereas on the curve the lower flange is right up against it. The curved track is shown canted as on the prototype; on a model curves are likely to be laid flat but the wheels on a model will still grind against the edge of the rail as it steers them round the curve. Which rail the flange presses against depends on the speed of the train – if lower than the speed the cant is designed to counteract then the weight of the train will press it against the lower rail, and if the speed is higher than the design speed centripetal force will press it against the higher rail. From a modelling point of view however, it is just important to note that the flange is pressed hard against the rail head, so any blips in this and you'll have trains running on the ballast.

against the rail, so a mis aligned joint where the next rail end juts out slightly into the gap between the rails has the potential to be disastrous, as the flange will ride up on the end of the rail, nip quickly across the top and fall off the other side. This quite often happens at insulated joints where the rails are held more loosely than they are with a metal fishplate, and the best way of avoiding this problem is simply to eliminate IBJs on curves. If that is impossible, and it transpires, on close examination of a derailment site, that a rail pokes out a bit into the four foot thus giving an end for a wheel to strike, then I tend to just file the rail end back a bit. If this kind of derailment is happening it generally only happens in one direction of traffic – in the other direction the wheel runs off the jutting out end and drops onto the next rail a little further behind.

FAULTS IN THE LEVEL OF THE TRACK - Twists

Twists are probably the biggest single cause of derailments on model railways and the least understood. They occur when one rail changes height relative to the other over a short length. They are essentially the same as super elevation or cant on a curve where one rail is raised slightly relative to the other, but over shorter lengths. Whereas cant gradually builds up and then down again, twists tend to be short, sharp and ugly. They are most common where one section of trackbase leads onto another at a slightly different angle.

Twists are especially good at derailing long wheel based unsprung four wheeled wagons or coaches. The longer the wheelbase the greater the potential problem as the vehicle will span far enough for one wheelset to be on and one off the twist, which results in one wheel hanging in space, with the rest of the vehicle supported on the other three wheels. The slightest discrepancy in alignment will then easily derail the train. Shorter wheelbases, for example bogies, generally just ride over twists, which is one of the reasons why bogie vehicles were so common in the States - they were the only thing that would run over some of their early trackwork.

Twists are usually easiest to spot by getting down on the ground and looking at the track. Looking across the track is best, where it is easy to see that the rear rail is lower than the near one. It is also possible to feel the effect of a twist by running a rigid four wheeled wagon or similar over the track and pushing slightly down. You can get a surprisingly accurate idea of the shape of the track from doing this – it also means you notice trouble spots where the track bends down under the passing wagon to give a bit of a dubious vertical alignment, but then springs back up again once it has passed, looking normal to the eye.

The best way to deal with twists is to alter the support under a section of track to eliminate them or at least, if they cannot be eliminated, to spread them out so they are not so sudden and therefore will not cause such a problem. The easiest way to do this if felt ballast has been

A twist in reality. The track crossing the foreground and going on across the diamond would win no 'Trackwork of the Month' prizes, but it is the rear line which is of specific interest – notice how the rail nearest the camera jerks up sharply just after the crossing, whereas the rail behind curves up gently, giving a terrible disparity in cross level – so bad it wouldn't fit on the measuring gauge. The shortness of the twist makes it perfect for derailing wagons, and you can be sure wagons running across, if they make it across this section of track at all without derailing, would do so on three wheels.

Using a four wheeled wagon to find a twist.

Not the ideal angle for a photograph, but it does demonstrate the process of spreading a twist out and thereby eliminating it. The couple of bits of felt on the right under the top rail tweak the track one way and the bit on the left at the bottom the other, counteracting the twist across the joint in the middle. Normally I would add these packing pieces under the 'ballast', making them a virtually invisible solution to the problem.

used is to add small bits of felt thereunder, or, if the felt is too thick, small sections of styrene sheet or similar. The additional bits of felt can be added under the ballast so they are not visible. In doing this you are generally turning the change in cross level from a twist to normal super elevation, which can be quite beneficial if the track properly builds up to it in both directions.

- Vertical Curves

Vertical curves are impossible to avoid at changes of gradient, but must be well thought out and actually a curve rather than a kink or they are likely to derail things like solid six wheeled vehicles which will rock over them. The easiest way to ensure changes of gradient occur as a curve rather than a kink is to lay a continuous piece of track over the point of change and not to pin it down too hard near the change point.

- Hammer Bent Rails

This is a problem which can arise in lengths of track which have been pinned down without the aid of a nail punch, and one or both of the rails has been bent by a blow from the hammer at the track laying stage. This results in a twist or vertical curve as explained above, which in certain situations can derail a train. Usually it is possible to spot places where this is a problem by eye; if not, a long straight edge laid along the rail will indicate fairly clearly where the problem is.

The easiest and best way to deal with this is to take the piece of track out complete and bend the rail back to straight. It can usually just about be bent back in situ, but this is less effective and more difficult to achieve.

FAULTS IN SWITCHES AND CROSSINGS

Switches and crossings, (S&C) are the most complex parts of railway trackwork and the area where the wheel is least guided - and consequently they are the places most prone to derailments. In many cases understanding the cause of a derailment in a junction situation can only be achieved by getting down on the ground with the offending vehicle and watching carefully the passage of the wheels through the problem area. Do not forget when investigating derailments in S&C that the part played by the back of the

A rail bent by slightly overenthusiastic use of a hammer. This has been exaggerated a bit and would be visible across the garden, but in more subtle cases the use of a straight edge can quickly highlight where the problem lies.

wheel is almost as important as that played by the front guiding a train; for example a derailment can occur if a check rail is not pulling a wheelset across to the correct side of a crossing.

After a few years outside the plastic sleepers of proprietary track often weaken a bit under exposure to UV light, and sometimes this creates problems at the tips of the switches, the couple of sleepers holding this end of a turnout together often breaking. The only way to overcome this really is to replace the turnout as once these timbers have failed the rest of the turnout is likely to follow fairly quickly, but you can change the couple of timbers here for copper clad ones almost between trains to keep things moving for a while.

In common with the prototype, a potential cause of derailments at turnouts is due not to the track itself but to misadjustment of the turnout operating device, be it manual or an electric point motor. Out in the garden you occasionally find that something has knocked part of the operating system out of alignment and bent a point rod, or that the rods themselves have expanded on a long length in the sun, meaning that the switch blades don't necessarily close right against the stock rail leaving a gap for a train in the facing direction to exploit and try to go up both routes at once. On the prototype the separate detection of both switch blades and the stretcher bar to a tolerance of a few millimetres makes sure it has all gone in the right direction, but this isn't so practical on a model. It is best just to bear in mind that you might want to check for this kind of fault if you discover that you get a repetitive derailment on a particular turnout. Don't forget that the point lever or motor will probably throw the point in a completely different way to you changing it with your finger – in fact it is amazing how points you'd think would never change work fine when given a hefty whack from a an old solenoid point motor.

Occasionally if platforms are surfaced in budgie grit or something similar bits of it walk over time, and can get stuck in turnouts and prevent them from throwing properly which creates the same problem, or even get stuck between rails in crossings or around checkrails. It is also worth checking for this problem if you keep getting derailments in the same place.

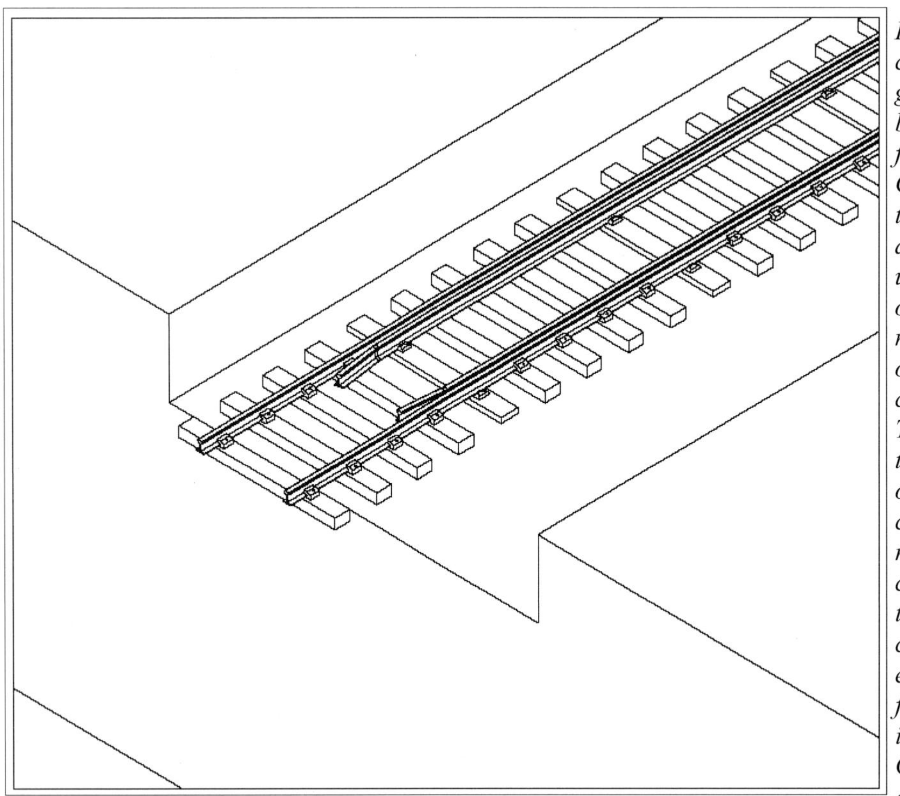

I've always found it more difficult to construct level crossings in the garden than for an 'inside layout' because outside they generally are functional rather than cosmetic. Certainly I have only ever installed them to get across garden paths, and whereas inside they can be built up out of cardboard and little strips of timber to form a visual representation of the real thing, outside they have to be more than capable of resisting errant feet.

To make the track a bit more solid therefore I tend to cut sections out of plastic trackbases and solder in copper-clad strip, which provides a much stronger joint than that from a cosmetic baseplate. Checkrails can then also be soldered to these copperclad sleepers, which are essential for preventing the concrete from filling up the flangeway on the inside of the rail.

Generally I find it easiest to cast the actual pathway one day, with a trench for the railway as shown in the drawing, and then come back and lay the track a couple of days later - this way you can lean on the path and are only trying to deal with a couple of inches of concrete before it sets, rather than a whole section of garden path. A relatively wet mortar mix can then be used to hold the track in position, tamping it in well under the sleepers. To aid track cleaning the rails want to eventually stand proud of the surface of the concrete by a fraction, but not so far that they snag on people's soles. It is also worth noting here that wet concrete reacts quite aggressively with nickel silver, which will result in the railheads going black as you cast the crossing - just come back and clean them a couple of days after the concrete has set; dry concrete is nothing like as reactive.

6

ELECTRICS

With any kind of model railway as soon as the track is down the desire to run something on it is virtually irresistible. Even for someone like me, who enjoys the wiring of the track, points and signals probably more than any other part of the construction process, it is particularly irritating that, once that line of metals is finally down, you still have to spend some time connecting various rails together and connecting up a supply before anything will run.

In the garden it is particularly important that the wiring is well thought out and installed. While a few bits of wire twisted together will get that first train running, they won't work at all after a winter contending with the weather. Voltage drop - a minor problem (if a problem at all) indoors - can become a real headache outside with the much longer lengths of wire inherent to garden railways, resulting in the trains getting slower and slower as they run along long sections, and outside it is also essential to bond every bit of rail together for successful operation. This may seem very tedious but, after trying to avoid doing it for years, I don't even bother trying to run trains over new trackwork before it is bonded up now – I just view bonding

A busy moment on Dr Bob Buckland's garden railway. The controller powering the whole affair can be seen on the left – the standard H and M unit so well known and loved by model railway builders, which plugs into an extension lead when the railway is in operation and lives inside when not. Wiring a line up like this works, of course, virtually infallibly, and those annoying little wiring faults which occasionally plague my operating sessions having limited potential for occurring here. *Photo: Dr Bob Buckland*

as an essential and integral part of the tracklaying process. If you skip it I guarantee you will get so fed up with jerky and spasmodic operation you will probably be tempted to pack the whole railway in through frustration.

Although I strongly recommend bonding up the track from the outset, the rest of the wiring can more or less entirely 'follow', and there is no need to completely wire the layout before getting those all-important morale boosting first trains running. My own layout worked off four wires for a long while, a supply to the controller and a supply to the track, the whole thing being bonded into one track section. Now, as I have mentioned before, the wiring connection listings run to many pages. This section looks at the various parts of the electrical system in the order that they become important during the installation process.

It is, in my opinion, worth doing things properly from the outset. After a couple of years you will have completely forgotten what you did when running a few quick supplies around the garden at the outset, and when it goes wrong you'll be forced into wholesale replacement rather than being able to mend a piece of a thought-out and well documented system. For similar reasons, I try to avoid wiring things up a bit here and a bit there, for example half the circuitry for a signal and leaving the other half to come later because I always find when I come back to it, possibly years later after something else has intervened, I can make neither head nor tail of either what I have done or the cryptic notes I left to finish the job with. This is especially true of circuits stretching across two control panels, or stretching miles down the garden – you'll just forget what you've done if you leave it half way through. If you're going to wire things up piecemeal, make sure you keep accurate records of exactly what you've done. Even complicated systems can be broken down into simpler circuits which can easily all be wired up at once.

Because of this gradual build up of the electrical system on most lines, it is imperative that a complete and up to date record is kept of what has been done. Personally I terminate all wires on tagstrip (of which more later) and keep records of what every connection does. This makes fault finding relatively straightforward. Most of the line is wired up in a fairly standard way, and if I wire something particularly out of the ordinary I will probably make a sketch of how I have done it. If I were starting from scratch I would probably keep proper wiring diagrams of the line – I have been avoiding doing this, partly out of laziness and partly because I couldn't honestly record all that exists after ten years of growth, but whenever I have a problem I always seem to find myself wishing I had.

ELECTRICITY SUPPLY

Whereas every railway requires a pile of transformers in the corner plugged into a multitude of adaptors and eventually into the mains, in the garden this becomes slightly more complicated as mains electricity and the great outdoors do not really mix. Unless you are operating your entire layout from inside, then you will have to supply electricity to a control panel somewhere in the garden, and it is by far preferable from a safety point of view to have only low voltage supplied to outside and the transformers located in the house, or possibly a well-built, dry shed. The transformers for my railway sit in the corner of the dining room, plugged in through an RCD and with a cut out on each circuit. The low voltage supply goes out through a hole drilled in the wall and is carried by some hefty cable in a conduit to the hut outside, from where it is distributed round the system. The actual controllers for a garden railway are exactly the same as those used for an inside line, as is most of the wiring, and I refer you to the many excellent books on the subject rather than giving an account of exactly how to wire the layout here.

As mentioned, some serious cable is required in the garden. I use 16/0.2 cable as standard – 16 strands of cable 0.2mm diameter, which is rated to about two amps, and I would not recommend anything smaller – indeed, for the low voltage ring mains round the garden I use some old mains flex which is considerably bigger.

You will get through an unimaginable amount of cabling in the garden, too, if you wire the railway up complete with individual track sections, point motors, signals and the like as opposed to the couple of wires which work perfectly for a line which is intended to only be a test track. I passed the mile mark years ago, and my

Some of the connections lists for my line are visible on the left in this photo, as usual in a handy position near the control panel for hasty resolution of those faults that seem to just love to occur when you've every siding full, two trains in the one loop and the block full in both directions. There is also a relay list recording what each set of contacts does and which other contacts they are linked to. During the wiring process I jot the data down by hand, typing it up at a later date. The typed up version is colour coded, in a similar way as the wiring itself, to try to aid the fault finding process.

The main power switches (ex RAF switches) and the ammeter for the various circuits on my garden railway. The ammeter can be connected across either 12v circuit, giving a quick indication of which one is causing problems.

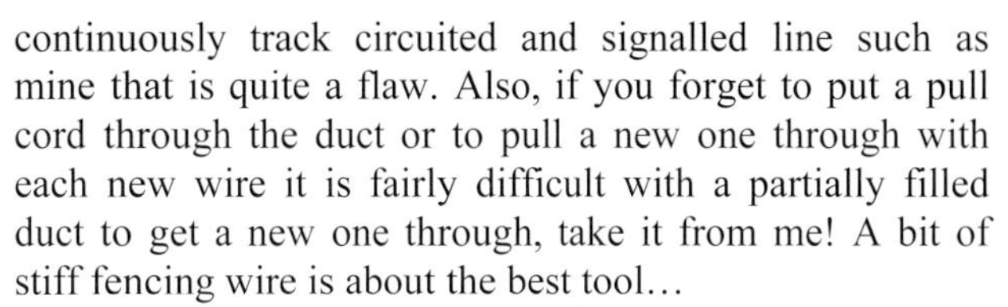

line is nothing compared to the scale of model empire the garden could provide the perfect home for.

Occasionally, of course, random wiring faults occur with any railway wiring, and this is no different in the garden – in fact the problem is compounded by the failure of soldered joints which happens slightly more often in the garden, so it is advantageous for individual supply circuits to be isolated at the distribution point and checked against an ammeter so you can tell by flicking a couple of switches which circuit the wiring problem lies on. A circuit drawing three amps, which normally doesn't draw enough to move the needle of the ammeter, is likely to be the first worth checking for a short circuit.

From the distribution point the supply needs to be run out to the various locations where it will be required. It makes life considerably easier if some thought is applied to the locations of the wiring runs right at the beginning of construction, as was mentioned in the 'planning' section. The wires can then be run along this route – either through a duct or just draped loose behind a wall or under a raised wooden trackbase.

I tend not to use ducts terribly much now as they are a bit restricting in where they go. You can't very easily take a few wires out half way along, and with a continuously track circuited and signalled line such as mine that is quite a flaw. Also, if you forget to put a pull cord through the duct or to pull a new one through with each new wire it is fairly difficult with a partially filled duct to get a new one through, take it from me! A bit of stiff fencing wire is about the best tool…

Wiring in the garden often involves running far greater lengths of cable than would be used on an inside layout, and the temptation to run all the wires to one location at once is considerable, even if it will be some time before they are used. I urge you to do this with caution however, making sure you know which wire is which at each end, either by terminating them all on a connector and recording the order or using individual cable identification tags, as on the prototype where all the wires are black. You also need to ensure that the ends of any wires or tagstrip connections which will not be used for a while are properly protected to prevent corrosion, which will happen fairly rapidly to any conductor left out in the open. This is easiest achieved by tinning both the wire and the tags on the tagstrips where exposed. The solder will tarnish, but the tarnish can easily be scraped off on a corner to get an iron against some clean solder, which will then quickly burn the rest of the surface corrosion off giving a

A corroded conductor which has been left in the open for far too long. It would be very difficult to connect another wire onto this – the wire will also be corroded on the inside, and the only way to joint into it would be to cut the wire and screw a connector in. I wouldn't recommend letting connections get this rusty – I took this photo during the re-signalling of Grogley Junction, and now all connections are in a solid, weatherproof enclosure. When using soldered connections it is usually possible to joint onto even the most corroded of joints as long as you can get enough heat to burn off the corrosion.

clean bit of solder to joint on to.

After a while the corrosion progresses up the inside of the cable, and if you cut a wire which has been in the garden for a long time you will find it very hard if not impossible to solder on to, even in the middle. In this case use a bit off a block of screw terminals to joint a length of new wire in, but don't expect to get it apart again after some time outside.

WEATHERPROOF CONNECTIONS

When running cables to a remote location out of the shelter or a hut or the house you will need some form of connector to terminate the wires on to. This is true of the wires running back from the track too, and the number of pins you need on these terminals grows and grows.

I terminate everything on tagstrips - I have gone away from using the 'chocolate block' style screw connectors as standard as the screws corrode rapidly outdoors - and a short wire connects the tagstrip to the socket into which plugs the control panel. The tagstrips and sockets I keep safe from the weather in a waterproof enclosure as plugs and sockets do not last very well outside, and will not survive more than a winter or two if left unprotected – I have the rusty sockets to prove it. I have some serious aluminium boxes mounted on posts with a rubber backing and a flap to keep the weather out of the bottom – since I started using these the connections have survived just as well as they would have had they been inside, and I would very much recommend a bit of outlay on some decent, weatherproof enclosures for wiring outside.

I find that soldered connections are the only ones which can be relied upon outside, and would not recommend building a line so far from an inside source of mains power that a soldering iron cannot be plugged in through an extension lead and an RCD and used to wire up the track. Twisting wires together might work for a few days but the wires are quick to oxidise outside, and the resistance of the joint will quickly build up, slowing trains down until eventually they work no more. The trouble then is that it will be a while since you quickly twisted a couple of wires together to solve a wiring fault, and you will have forgotten where you did it, and which circuit you need to fix, and it all goes downhill from there really!

CONTROL PANELS IN THE GARDEN

It would of course be possible to have the controls for any garden line inside, but I would try to dissuade people from doing this – as, while it makes life easier not requiring the control panel to be removable or weatherproof, it means someone is more or less tied to sitting inside with the controls to prevent a disaster if a wheel of a train becomes derailed, which is not much fun for them. Garden railway building is an outdoor activity, and sitting in the garden running trains is an extremely pleasant pastime. For the sake of a few extra plugs and

One of the control panels in use on my garden railway. The other is shown in the Operation and Stock section, which works in conjunction with the signalling diagram shown in the next section.

sockets, it is well worth allowing everyone to partake in this enjoyment.

I also very much enjoy running my railway with two operators – something few of us have the space to achieve inside but which in the garden can be relatively easily arranged. The number of control panels you need will depend on the geographical setup of your line and will be different for every system, and to an extent depends on the number of operators you can manage to cajole into helping you run the railway. All of my track sections are wired along 'cab control' principles, meaning they can all be operated from either station, so the whole line is able to be operated by just one person.

Whether or not you require a control panel in the garden is entirely dependent on what you want to get out of the railway you have built and how much you enjoy wiring model railways, a situation no different to that found indoors. The simplest option is to have a single controller feeding one track section, which can be arranged with a few lengths of wire and a simple socket in a weatherproof

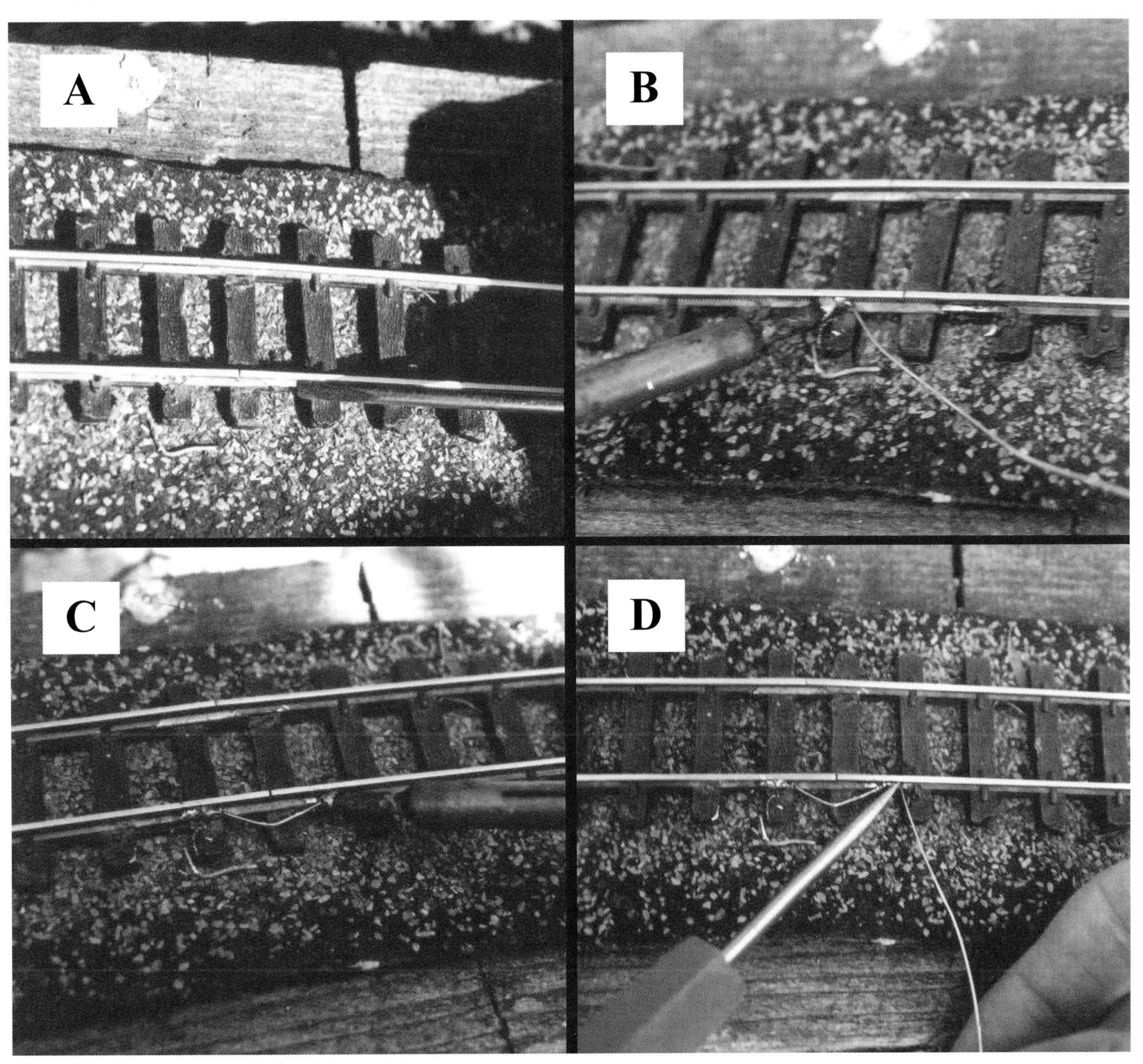

The procedure I use for bonding up the track. The first step (A) is to strip the insulation off the wire so you have one long, un-insulated strand. The two rails then need to be cleaned off – I use an electrical screwdriver to scrape the oxidisation off the rail. The two rails are then tinned as is the end of the wire, and the wire soldered onto one rail (B). The wire is then given a kink in the middle around the end of the iron to give some flexibility if the rail moves, and then soldered onto the other rail (C). I then break the rest of the wire off by waggling it under the screwdriver blade (D) – it soon breaks, and it's on to the next joint. The whole process takes seconds – genuinely less time than reading this.

place as mentioned above. Should control panels be required in the garden, their actual guise is again open to individual taste and they are no different to those built inside, apart from the fact that all the electrics will have to be contained in the one panel which it should be possible to move inside. That said, I have some track circuits and points relays located in remote location cabinets, but if you are going to do this make sure they are truly weatherproof boxes. Control of points and signals is discussed in a later chapter.

BONDING THE TRACK

As I mentioned in passing earlier, it is vital that all rails are bonded together electrically. Any kind of wire can be used, but it is essential that it is soldered to both rails. Through attaching hundreds of bonds in my life I have developed the process illustrated for bonding up the track.

I use the single solid-core wire found in telephone or networking cable as it is easy to shape and solder as required, and for the locos I run this is perfectly adequate in terms of ability to convey current. I would imagine it would be fine for anything up to an amp or so – beyond this kind of current draw some heavier wire might be required. This wire also tarnishes in time, along with the solder, to give an unobtrusive joint.

It is important to remember to bond round switches and crossings to ensure every rail is fed with track current. It soon becomes apparent if it isn't as you'll hear the engines falter as they go over an unbonded bit of rail. Sometimes these bonds drop off after a winter, which is apparently due to migration of the tin atoms during winter when there is no flow of electrons – if this has happened, just solder on a new bond. I use the same wire to attach track feeds to the track, as once it has tarnished it is significantly less obtrusive than a great piece of 16/0.2 wire soldered to the track. The heavier wire is soldered to the thin single core wire under the trackbed.

A piece of thin, ex-telephone wire taking the track feed down to below the trackbase, where the heavier and less sightly wire is connected on. The line here, on top of the viaduct, is track circuited so both rails are fed – the other feed is behind and runs under the plastic sleepers to the other rail. If feeding both rails with bare wires like these it saves a lot of time searching for faults if you make sure they can't touch and short out, which always seems to be the last thing I think to check. I usually reduce the likelihood of this happening by connecting the wires to the rails either side of a sleeper rather than in the same bed.

7

S & T - POINT AND SIGNAL OPERATION

It is, of course, entirely possible to build a garden railway which will give you many years of enjoyment without any signals, point motors or similar complications, but personally one of my favourite garden railway building tasks is wiring up signals and turnouts and watching them work from afar, signal aspects changing as the trains go by.

For a while I had some hand worked turnouts using the 'slot in tube' style of point lever employing a diagonal slot across a bit of thick walled tube to give the required linear movement. A sketch of this arrangement is given below.

POINT MOTORS

Although not necessarily a priority while a line is in its infancy point motors are, in my opinion, very desirable on a garden railway. They significantly reduce the amount of moving around an operator has to do in much the same way as inside, the difference in the garden being the scale of the moving involved. Whereas inside either end of a loop may be six feet or so apart, in the garden this can be 16 feet even in a small scale. The space available in the garden allows for an expansion of the layout which is one of the great advantages of it as somewhere to build a railway, but in so doing it greatly increases the amount of exercise the line provides.

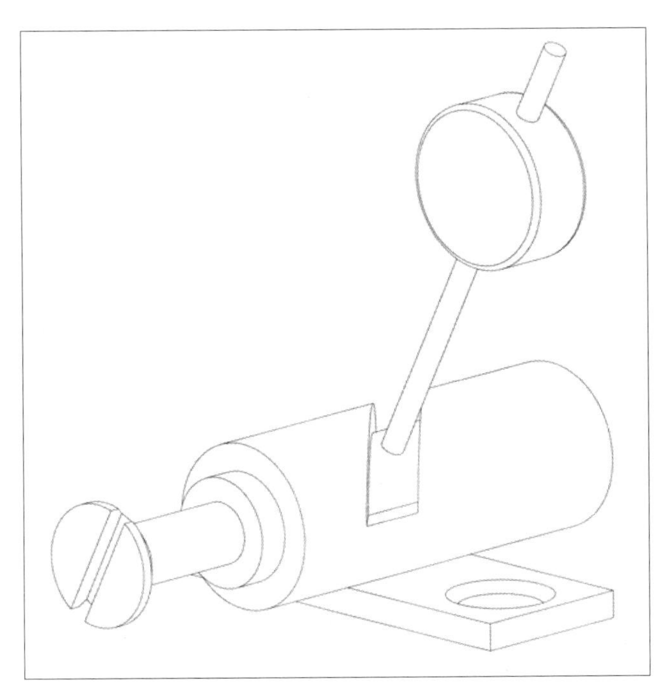

A manual point lever which I have used successfully in the past. The screw at the end is needed to stop the whole point rod twisting as you change the points.

Most people, me included, baulk initially at the price and added complication of point motors, but in time the temptation to 'just add those points to the box' creeps up on you for the far-flung turnouts, and eventually you hardly install a turnout before its associated motor is connected up. Another advantage of turnout motors is that they provide an easy way to mount turnout operated switches if 'electrofrog' crossings are used - I would not, through experience, trust the bond of a switch against the relevant stock rail to give electrical conductivity every time it is thrown. The bond works fairly well for a while but after a winter and some serious oxidisation the reliability will dramatically reduce. As an extension to the general laziness theory expounded for the introduction of turnout motors in the first place, it is annoying to have to keep getting up to push a loco over the same turnout time and time again. I therefore fit switches to change the crossing polarity as standard to all 'electrofrog' turnouts.

If you must use the actual motor-operated type of point motors available make sure they are extremely well insulated from the elements. I have always used solenoid motors, and know of several other people who have had no problems with them over prolonged periods outside, especially the older H and M type.

As long as they are looked after point motors will work relatively happily year after year if mounted on top of the baseboard next to the track, which is by far the easiest way of mounting them. Common is the PECO type of point motor. In this arrangement a mounting plate (PL9) is screwed to the board, the motor mounted on this and the relevant switch (usually PL13) stuck to the top of it with evostick. The term point 'motor' stems from the prototype – they use a similar system to the motor operated versions for a garden railway.

A length of brass wire is used wrapped around the pin of the motor to transfer the drive and, in the case of a PECO turnout, wrapped also around the end of the tiebar. The drive need not be direct and can be taken around a number of cranks or equalisers.

I have quite a few cranks seen in some of the photographs - they need a drop of oil every now and again but generally work well. Critical for successful turnout operation when routing the drive round a number of cranks is that the losses in each individual crank are minimised, so about the

An M3 type point motor on the real thing, in this case at Smallbrook Junction on the Isle of Wight. The motor is the black bit on the left in the foreground, beyond it in the bolted down cover lies the gearbox and crown wheel which actually provide the drive to the switches (exiting on the left), and beyond that lie the detection switches. These are operated by the three smaller rods entering from the left, one each for the switches and one for the stretcher bar, and they make or break the eight individual contacts clearly visible. The outermost pair of contacts on each side deals with stopping the motor as it approaches the end of its wind, and the inner four are all wired in one circuit, so if all the bits are in the right place current flows and a relay changes in a nearby location cabinet to do things like prove signal routes and provide an indication on the panel of what the points are doing on the ground.

same amount of movement occurs at the actual tiebar as is provided by the point motor. It is to minimise the losses of movement that my standard design of crank uses nuts and bolts to hold the thing firmly as it rotates - I find these very successful at providing a firm but freely moving pivot. Proprietary parts can, of course, be used such as the 'Gem' cranks.

The size of wire used is essentially down to personal preference, I have found 0.45mm wire perfectly adequate on fairly long runs to work 0-16.5 turnouts. The most important feature in actually getting the points over is the force applied by the centre-over spring – if this is working well, holding the point blades tight against the stock rail, the turnout will throw successfully every time even with only a little movement from the rodding. It can't be so tight it stops the motor from throwing however – a balance is needed.

It is, of course, possible to mount the motors below the track as done inside – this is aesthetically slightly more pleasing, but ensure that the water can drain from the hole in which it is mounted - a sure way to wreck a motor is to sit it in water all winter.

A small crank suitable for changing the direction of a turnout operating rod. The challenge in getting these to work is in minimising losses of motion, and to this end I now generally attach the operating rods through another smaller nut and bolt arrangement, eradicating any slack arising from the rod moving in the hole.

Point motors are wired up in exactly the same way outside as inside – just make sure you use some good heavy wire. A capacitor discharge unit is not absolutely essential but makes a big difference, as inside, in persuading those sticky motors over, especially if more than one motor is operated at once - for example if both parts of a crossover are on separate motors.

When it comes to the type of switch used to operate the motor, the same options as used inside are again possible – some kind of indication of the state of a turnout outside is useful however, so the passing contact lever type switches which have been manufactured by various people over the years are particularly good as they give a permanent visual indication of the state of the line.

Point motors are generally used in the garden for far-flung and difficult to access turnouts, so it can be virtually impossible to see if they have actually thrown or not. This is the main reason why some form of detection at the turnout is desirable though, like point motors themselves, not essential. A few trains sent the wrong way and into the back of other ones tends to focus the mind, however, on working out an indicator system.

The switch mounted on the motor can of course be used for this, connected directly to some bulbs, although in many cases there is more than one thing which you will want to switch with a turnout, for example the crossing polarity, the panel indicators and the route on a signal. It can be useful, therefore, to wire up a relay for at least some of the turnouts. Relays are essentially just switches but instead of being mechanically actuated they are worked by an electromagnet. They can be wired with a feed from a 12v ring main round the garden to one side of the detecting switch and the switched supply taken back to the panel in which the relays can be situated in an environment where they don't have to deal with the weather. It is not essential to connect the relays immediately - they can, for example,

The 7-lever frame which controls most of the points at one of my stations. It started as an MSE frame, but has been very much modified to create something slightly more akin to the prototype. This is virtually all brass, with the exception of a spring to return the catch handles, and if these were omitted I would imagine it could be quite happily left outside screwed to the base and used to mechanically operate the points. I have added switches to the lever tails however, and it electrically works all my points and is built into the actual control panel. I suppose technically, therefore, all the levers should be shortened as the end two are to denote electrical working, but somehow it looks better as it would be in the box with the ones in the middle still yet to be cut down. The only slight problem with a lever frame such as this is that there is no indication, apart from a few cryptic notes on the lever plates, of which lever does what – a diagram is needed.

follow with the signalling at a later date, and initially the switch on top of the point motor can be connected up at the lineside to work the crossing polarity, which is essential to the all-important task of getting those first trains running.

It is also possible to use sprung microswitches, but the springing of these can be fairly fierce and can act against the over-centre spring holding the tiebar in position with sufficient force to push the switch rail away from the stock rail, which will result in a derailment in the facing direction. Another option which overcomes this is the use of a radio style switch. These push on, push off switches have quite a few contacts down the side and can provide a useful little multi-pole sliding switch if the mechanism which provides the click is removed. Unfortunately they don't deal so well with the weather, although they will give you switching of multiple circuits at the lineside for a while before corroding.

On the prototype, the round repeaters on the block

Use of prototype repeaters. Those with coils marked 1,500 ohms each work well on 12v – leave the link at the top in place and connect onto the two screws at the bottom, as here. Repeaters for signals tend to be around 300 ohms in total and 12v will fry them – you need about a volt and a half, no more.

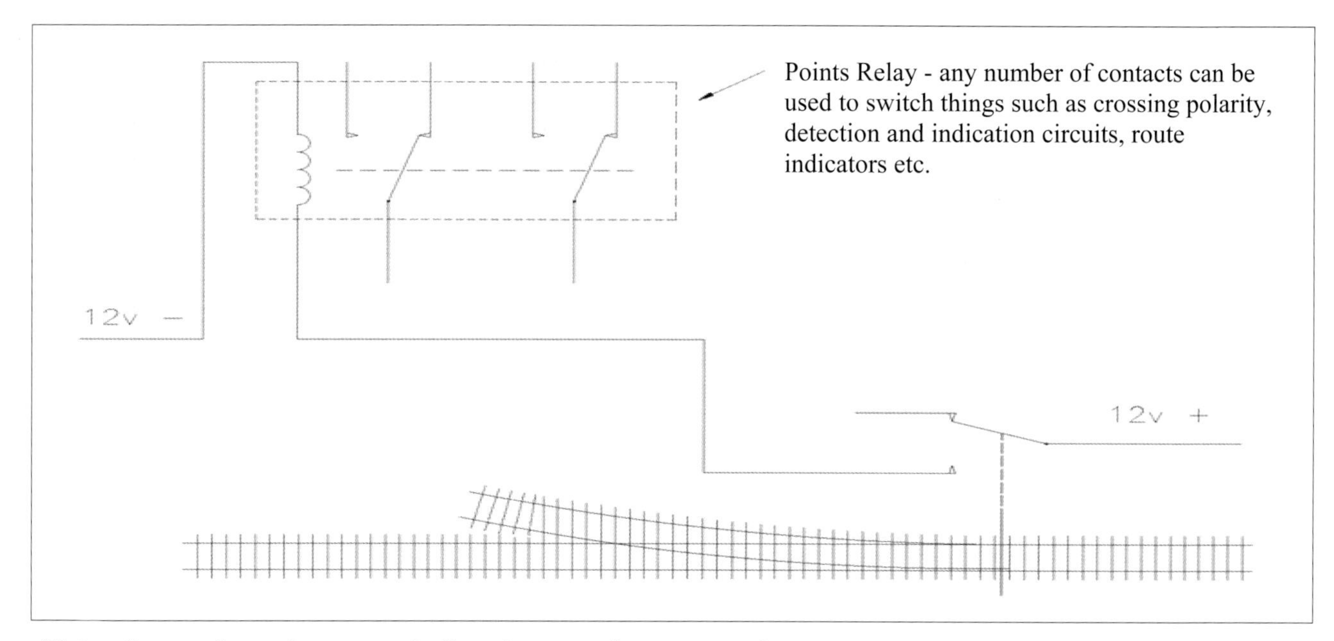

Wiring diagram for a relay operated off a point motor detection switch.

shelf of the signal box indicate the state of turnouts out of view from the signal box. If these can be found they give an impressive and realistic indication of the state of the turnout - there's nothing more like the prototype than using bits from the prototype, but they are quite hard to source and almost impossible to make, I have decided after years trying. They need to be wired with a two-wire supply which switches polarity, achieved most easily through a relay, to change the indication from normal to reverse. No current gives a 'wrong' indication.

MAINTAINING POINT MOTORS

Solenoid motors have an element of steel in them and the switches can be on the delicate side for what you want to leave open to the elements all year. Never underestimate the destructiveness of the weather. It is desirable therefore to cover the motors if possible, and this is something to bear in mind when planning the layout of the railway in relation to the buildings around it. A small building is the easiest way to protect a point motor. Signal boxes, relay cabinets etc are particularly useful prototypes as in reality they are commonly found near turnouts. Many motors can be grouped under one cover and the rodding run from the covering building to the actual point ends. In the case of a double junction, or a scissors crossover where there are a lot of point ends in one area this is a useful way of reducing the number of little buildings you have to build! The actual construction of small buildings is covered in the next chapter.

It is important that these buildings are easy to move as from time to time it is essential to oil the motors. WD40 is good as it is easy to direct and moisture repellant; 3 in 1 is also good and thicker, staying in one place for longer, but will float on top of water. It is important to give the motor itself a good dousing but try to avoid the switch ,as oil on the contacts won't help the electrical connection between the various parts of the switch.

The over centre spring in the turnout itself also needs attention from time to time. Electrolube, as recommended by PECO, is best. Oiling the motors a couple of times a winter is usually enough, working the points as you do so to make sure the oil gets into all the places likely to rust.

A small building covering the point motor for the turnout beside it. This is based on a French relay cabinet – there are many UK buildings which could be modelled in the same location – the railways seemed to love huts.

SIGNALLING

When building a line such as the garden allows, with stations far apart and linked by prototypically long stretches of main line, signalling is something which takes on a whole new dimension. Signals are not purely there for aesthetic reasons (although they do look very impressive), but rather can be situated prototypical distances apart and made to actually control the trains. They can also form a useful means of communication between signal boxes or stations when they are under separate control. Admittedly a little effort is required to set up a signalling system, but it is a process I personally enjoy immensely and a great deal of satisfaction can be derived from seeing it all working, especially from afar when someone else is operating it or, best of all, when it is operating itself.

A signalling system is, like point motors and so much else, something which can be left 'to follow', and can be more or less ignored during the initial construction of the line when there is so much else to do, but it provides a task which can create ongoing construction work for years if actually building the line interests you more, perhaps, than operating it.

THE SIGNALS THEMSELVES

There are two main types of signal: mechanical and colour light. While colour lights are easier to build and wire, both inside and outside, there is no contest with the grace of a semaphore signal in terms of appearance – an appearance only enhanced outside.

Once the layout has been determined the actual signalling design can be worked out. The best way of approaching this is to find a prototype with the same - or a similar track layout, and use the signalling from there. If actually carrying out signalling design it is worth looking at other situations to try to understand the mentality behind prototype signalling design. As with most railway-orientated things, there is common sense and logic behind it, with safety - as ever - the driving force behind decision making. Signalling is designed to 'fail safe', i.e. that is if a failure does occur the state to which the system reverts will be a safe one and will not suddenly set up conflicting moves. An example is the balance weight on a signal - if the wire snaps this will return the signal to danger by its own weight and will thereby prevent trains from running past it. It is also important to understand that while everything to do with signalling is installed to a very high standard and maintained in a very strictly regimented way, cost was always a factor in design and signalling tended to be very efficient. The design would give enough flexibility for routes which would be realistically used, but not signal every possible route purely for the sake of it in the hope it might be used one day. Layouts were developed to work in a particular way, and signalled with this in mind.

A conservative approach can be taken to laying out signals in the garden. It is difficult, for example, to see shunt signals, especially semaphore ones outside, and these can be left out of the signalling design altogether if desired. I tend to use colour light shunt signals where I use them at all.

Signals can be constructed and operated in a similar manner to that used for inside models - however it is important to bear in mind that, if not removable, they will have to contend with the winter, which is a fairly destructive force. This is a particular problem in the case of semaphore bracket signals including small cranks.

On balance then the removable option is preferable. If electrically operated this can easily be achieved with a plug and socket arrangement. I make signals of all kinds in brass, soldered together - as well as being robust this allows the return path for any bulbs to be through the body of the signal. In my experience wooden posts are so small that they rot far too fast to be worth using outside.

It is possible, of course, to build non-working models of signals for garden railways – these are much easier to construct and require none of the control systems associated with working signals. It is also possible that there won't be either the time or the funds to build and connect up all the signals when building the signalling system initially, in which case the signals can be built to work but installed as aesthetic features only, being wired up properly at a later date, which is usually the way signals get installed on my line. It is the work of a few minutes to wedge the operating rods on semaphore signals until such time as I can afford the solenoids, or in the case of colour light signals hooking up a couple of wires directly to the main low-voltage supply when the signal is initially installed to illuminate a proceed aspect, with the relays and track circuits and similarly complicated control gear following at a later date.

When building signals for use on a garden line it is, as with most things, not essential for them to be exactly to scale. Far more important is that the proportions of the signal are right. To allow for the use of LES bulbs therefore, which give a good focused beam, I make all signals to a scale of roughly 7.5mm:ft for my otherwise nominally 7mm:foot scale line.

SEMAPHORE SIGNAL CONSTRUCTION

A single arm on a post is, of course, easiest to build, but bracket signals are not significantly more difficult. The only slight challenge is in making cranks which work sufficiently well, as the losses through the joints that plague cranks in point rodding runs are equally problematical with signals. The nut and bolt approach can be employed again here, but I find such pivots can be a bit visually intrusive on the face of signal brackets. The wire-in-tube approach as shown in the exploded diagram - a

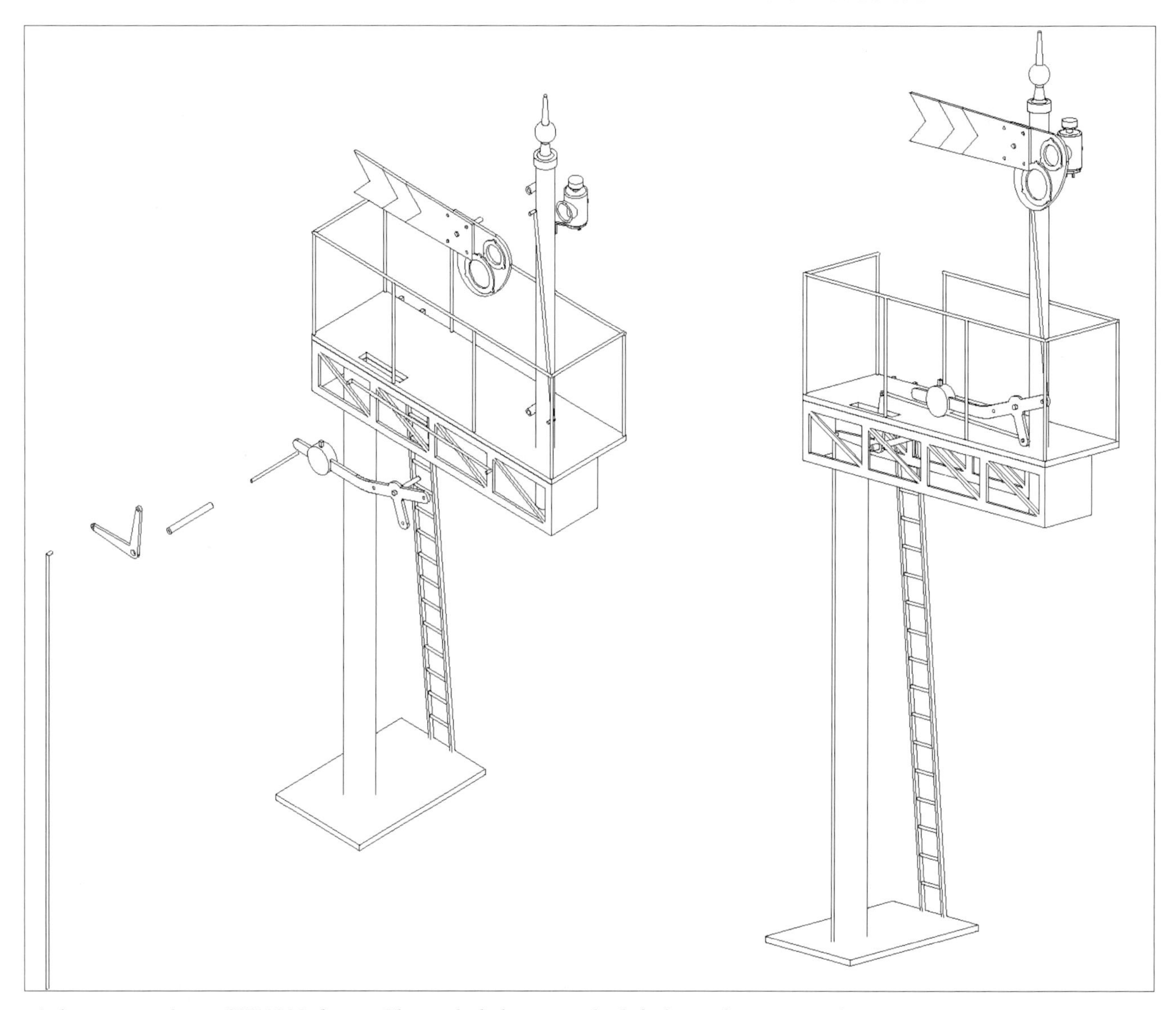

A distant signal to a GW 1928 design. The exploded view on the left shows the wire in tube pivot arrangement I use extensively, and the balance weight and arm are all pivoted on using the same arrangement. The crank is soldered onto a bit of wire which pivots in the close-fitting tube soldered to the bracket. Signals like this can be built up from proprietary parts as you would inside, including cast finials and lamp housings.

length of tube soldered to the crank turning on a close-fitting piece of wire attached to the bracket, works equally well as long as there is a good length of brass wire in the tube to give a sufficiently large bearing area and hold the crank square.

It is well worth adding working lights to semaphores; they look fantastic outside at night. A grain of wheat bulb is ideal, or if desired a white LED can be used – these, although slightly more expensive, will virtually never blow, meaning you'll never have to rebuild part of a signal to change the lamp as can occasionally be a problem with grain of wheat bulbs. LEDs also don't give off heat, so a whitemetal housing can be used without the danger of melting inherent in using grain of wheat bulbs, although to avoid this problem when using grain of wheat bulbs I generally cut the whitemetal base off the lamp casting and substitute a bit of brass tube which is a bit more resistant to the heat, super gluing the cast top back on top of the tube. Mounting the bulb or LED upright in the lamp housing means it is also possible to have the backlight working on the signal (the small white aspect to the rear) – this is another one of those little things which makes a big difference to the overall effect.

COLOUR LIGHT SIGNAL CONSTRUCTION

If making colour light signals it is best to use filament lamps as opposed to LEDs. Although easier to use in some respects and longer lasting, LEDs are not as bright as filament bulbs and consequently are harder to see outside in direct sunlight. Colour light signals in '0' gauge or thereabouts can be built with 'LES' bulbs to form the

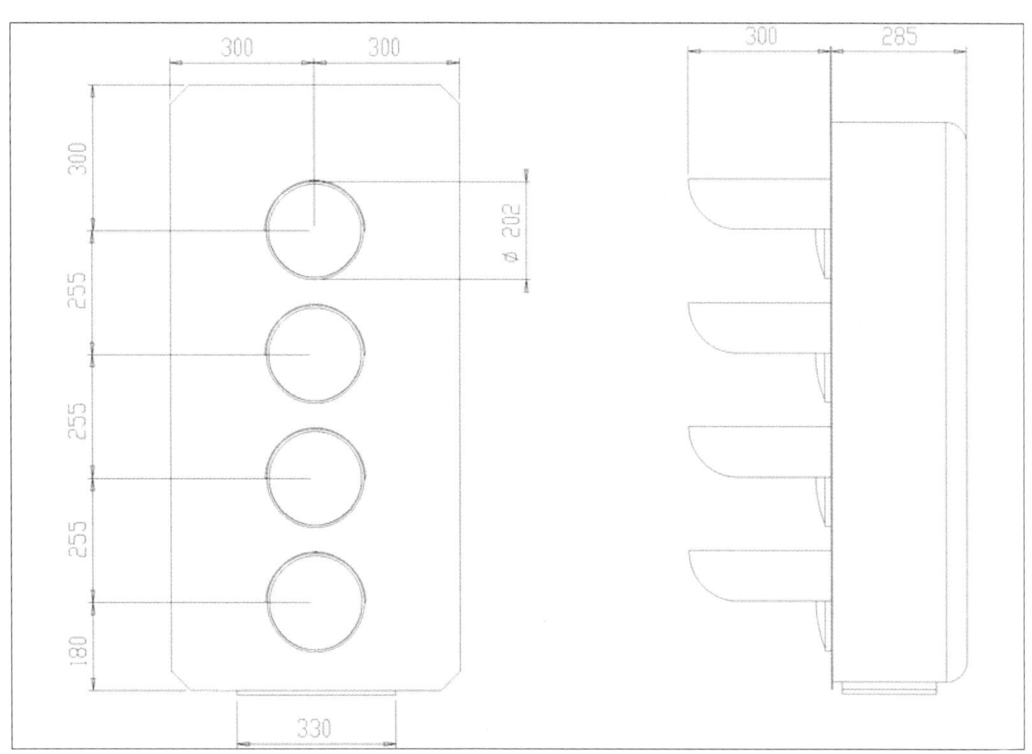

A BR standard signal head drawing. For signals of fewer aspects knock out one of the middle ones, the edge distances are always the same. While model colour light signals, such as those from the Eckon range, often have curved tops these are few and far between on the prototype – those at Honiton on the Salisbury – Exeter line are the only ones that I can think of. This square edged design is by far the most prolific, albeit less attractive to look at.

aspect which are coloured using acrylic stained glass paint, the same paint as used to colour the spectacle glass in semaphores. LES bulbs are small filament bulbs with a lens at the end which gives an accurately focused beam. Signals for smaller scales can make effective use of grain of wheat bulbs – I find the Expo ones are particularly good at giving a clear bright light.

It is important to try to find a good colour for signal aspects, as some of the transparent paints which can be bought look very similar. I use an emerald green to give the fairly bluish green of a signal, a very bright lemon yellow to give a well-defined yellow colour and a crimson paint for red. To get a good deep red colour it can be necessary to add an extra coat of paint in comparison with the other colours.

When using directional bulbs such as the LES bulbs it is important to get them all pointing in the same direction. I achieve this by holding the bulbs gently in a vice as I solder them to the signal face plate.

Through many failed attempts at constructing signals resulting in aspects pointing off in all sorts of skewiff directions, I have developed the procedure shown above for soldering up colour light signal heads. The bulbs are loosely held in the vice – the jaws just touching the bulbs and not putting any pressure on them at all – and the face plate of the signal laid on top of the vice and soldered to them. Once the bulbs have been accurately aligned as shown the rest of the signal can be easily fabricated in brass.

MOUNTING SEMAPHORE SIGNALS

I tend to mount signals on a Perspex base and screw them to separate supports of two by one inch timber in the same way as point motors. If mounted beside the track on a wall the supports can, of course, be screwed to the wall. Semaphore signals can be worked by point motors mounted vertically or solenoids which act in only one direction and use gravity as a means of return.

The solenoid method is simpler as only one wire is required in addition to an earth and the switching is easier in the control panel, but then solenoids tend to be more

The solenoid working the signal described. This pulls the armature up, pulling the arm off, and a spring, gravity and the blob of bluetack (very useful for holding the signal for the photo) return it to danger. The brass tube across the way at the top holds the pin which keeps the cover in place. The operating arm is soldered to the bit of connector block, which is slid up and down the armature to adjust the angle of dangle of the signal arm itself. A cover (essential) will keep the weather off the armature and then this signal is ready for screwing in place. Three wires, clearly labelled, will connect to those buried in the ground, also labelled, through a soldered joint so they can easily be un-soldered again should the signal require a bit of adjustment or to allow it to be taken inside for the winter.

expensive in comparison with point motors. Point motors have the advantage that a standard point motor switch can easily be mounted on the types of motor which do not include them as standard (such as the Seep motors), and this can be useful to repeat the signal on the panel or can be used to control a distant or a route indicator or similar signal which only works when the main arm is off.

Having said that, if you control a solenoid through a relay in the control panel you can just use extra contacts on the signal relay to detect the aspect of the signal, and a separate detection switch out on the ground becomes unnecessary unless you are particularly worried about indicating exactly the state of the arm.

The final decision depends on whether you want to opt for slightly cheaper and slightly more weather resistant point motors or easier to wire solenoids.

To mount things like PECO point motors vertically the fact that the common side of the two coils is connected together can be exploited, and a mounting bracket soldered to the two tags to provide a secure mounting for the motor, which in turn can be screwed to the underside of the Perspex base plate with a bolt in a tapped hole. A bit of brass wire wrapped around the pin of the point motor and you're in business.

MOUNTING COLOUR LIGHT SIGNALS

A Perspex base also makes a good foundation on which to mount colour light signals. Attached to the underside of the Perspex mounting plate is a length of tagstrip or connector block to allow removal of the signal for testing if required, and then the signal is wired back to the control panel. Either single cores or multicore cable can be used multicore is easier but it tends to be white which sticks out like a sore thumb across a garden. It can be turned brown to a degree by covering it in creosote, but the effect of this wears off after a while outside.

MECHANICAL CONTROL OF SEMAPHORE SIGNALS

The simplest way of operating a semaphore signal, as with turnouts, is to use a length of string and a weight. If this mechanical link method is used it is most effective with some kind of man-made string such as fishing line, which is completely non elastic and therefore won't stretch. It is also a low friction material and can easily be passed through hooks and eyes to change direction. At the signal end some kind of weight is used to hold the line taught and return the signal to danger, and at the operational end a large number of options could be pressed into service - a full lever frame following prototype practice for example, either a self manufactured one or one purchased commercially – the latter is possibly the best but, of course, also the most expensive option.

If something more straightforward is desired a simple handle with an ability to be locked in the 'off' position can be used. The major drawback with these

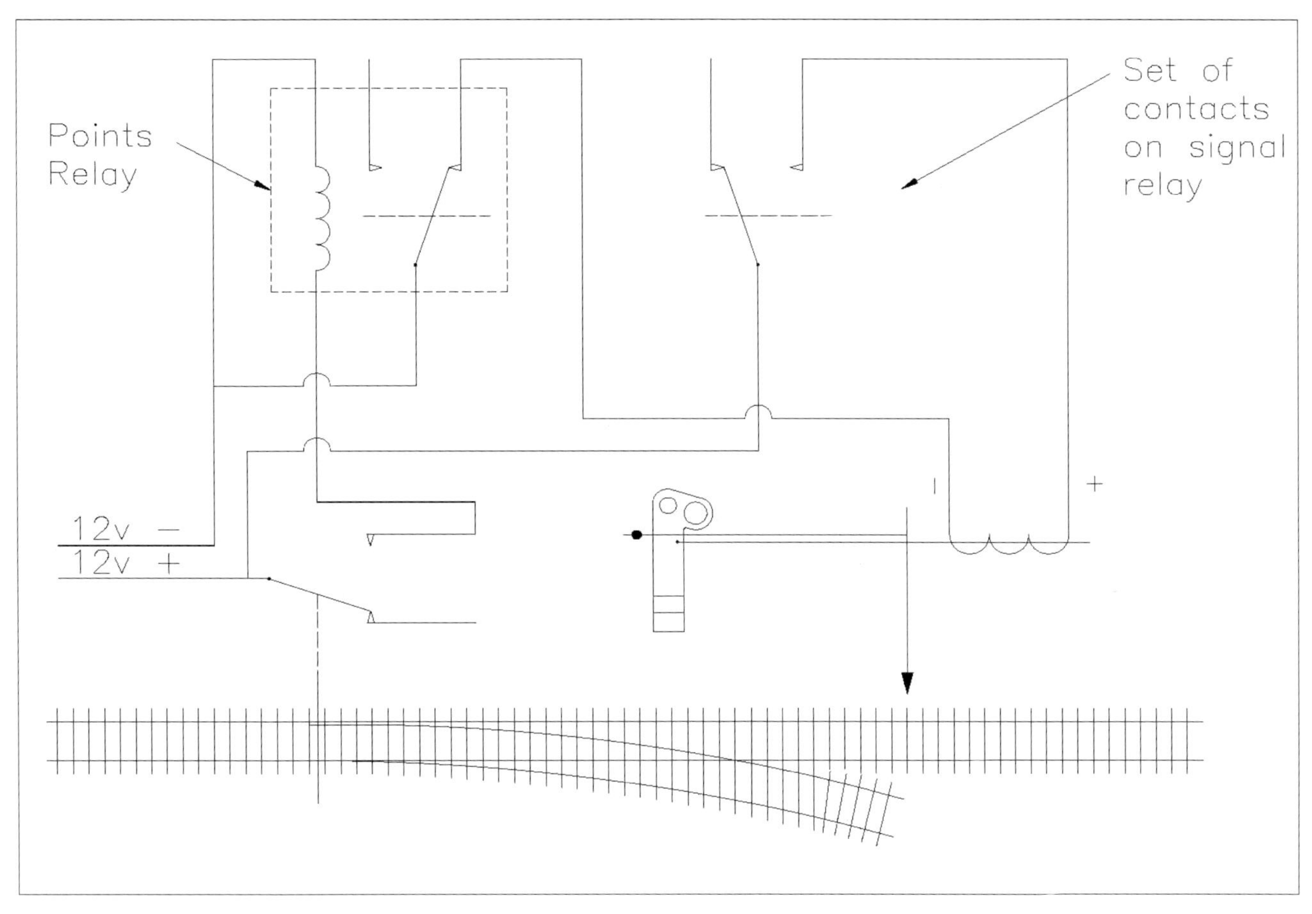

Interlocking a solenoid operated signal with the route it applies to. If you follow the wiring to the solenoid on the left the positive side is switched through the signal switch or signal relay in the normal fashion, but the negative return side is switched through a contact on the points relay. Current will only flow through the solenoid coil when the point is set the right way, and the signal will return to danger if the points are reversed in front of it. This is something which can be easily arranged with a solenoid but is quite difficult with a point motor operated signal, as with a point motor the current only flows for a fraction of a second.

systems is that they all have to be outside all of the time – you can't plug in the operational end as you can with an electrical switch. The options for further control, such as track circuit control or interlocking with the block system are also reduced.

ELECTRICAL CONTROL OF SEMAPHORE SIGNALS

It is easy to control semaphore signals electrically in the garden and also to make electrically operated semaphores removable, to avoid the winter destroying them. If using point motors to work the arms the wiring is exactly the same as for a turnout, and even simpler in the case of a solenoid when only one wire is required from the panel, along with a common return. A passing contact switch in the case of a point motor or a standard toggle switch can be used to work the signal on the panel, or indeed a lever frame with electrical switches attached to the lever tails instead of physical rodding.

The chief advantage of electrical control is that it allows easy interlocking of the signals, for example with the turnouts so a route cannot be signalled through a turnout which is not set right. This is only really possible with solenoid operated signals.

COLOUR LIGHT SIGNALS

Wiring colour light signals is very simple; the circuit is no more complicated than wiring a torch. It is shown overleaf for three aspect signals which can be easily extended to any situation. The signals can be simply controlled by toggle switches on the panel either laid out geographically or in a lever frame arrangement.

The arrangement(A) overleaf works well with signals controlled by the same panel, when the line wires (the three with arrows on in the diagram) only have to stretch to the next switch, but life becomes a lot more complicated when the signals are controlled by panels a long way apart. Long lengths of wire are required in

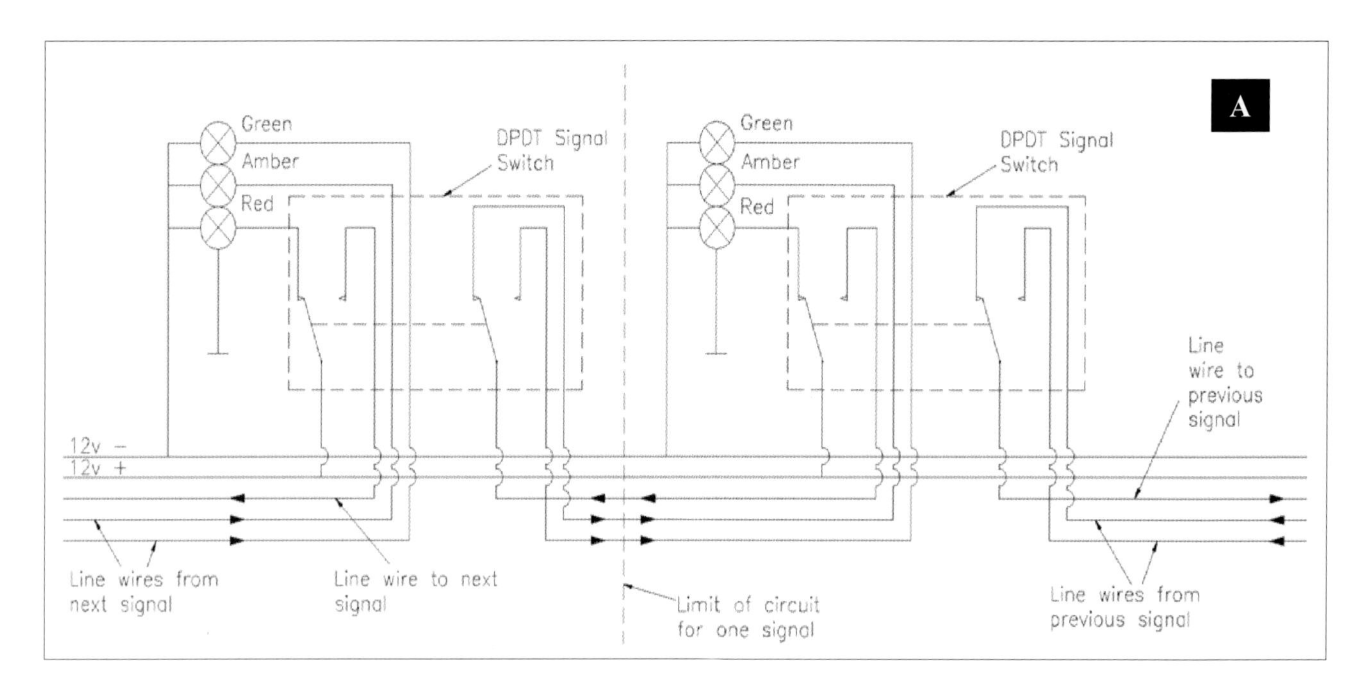

Switched control for consecutive colour light signals down a single track, single direction line – for example either the up or down line on a section of double track.

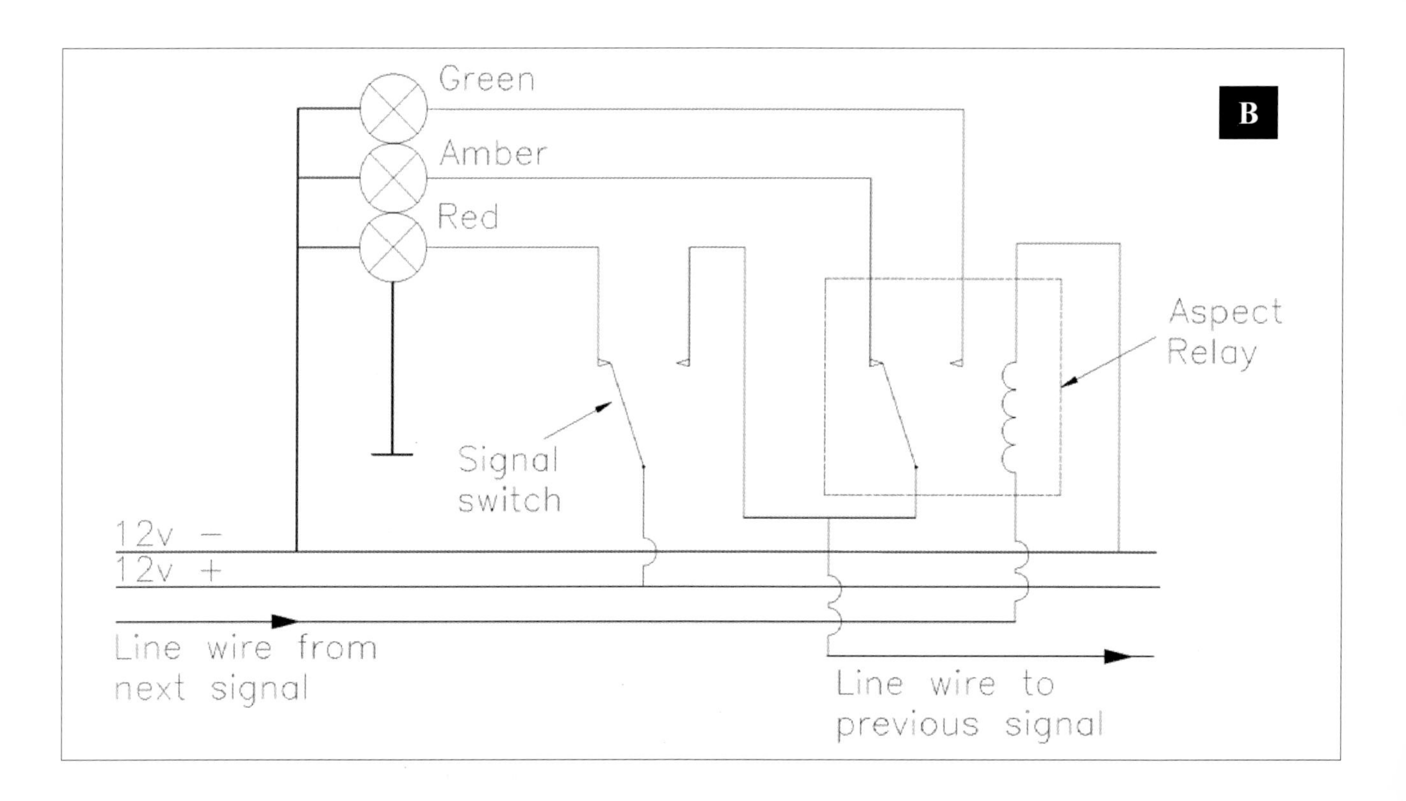

Control of colour light signals by aspect relays.

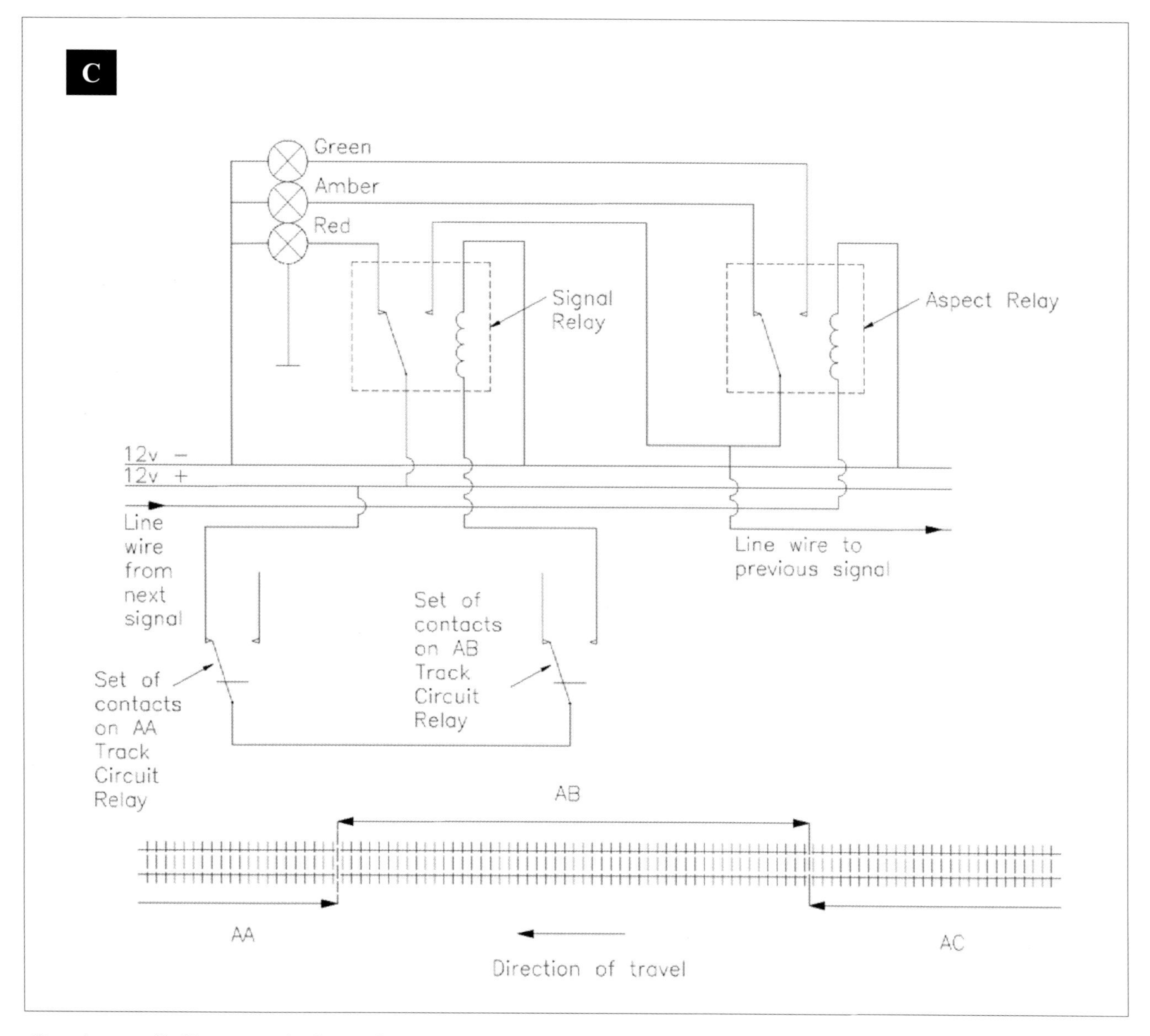

Signal controlled by a signal relay and aspect relays. In this case the switch above has been substituted for the signal relay, which allows for a whole range of possibilities in terms of signal control. In this case contacts on the track circuit relays for the appropriate sections are used to work the signal. A train occupying AB track circuit will clear the signal to the appropriate aspect, it returning to red as track circuit AA is occupied. A system of signals doing this laid out round the garden looks fantastic working all on its own, more than repaying the hours spent installing the system. If getting involved in track circuits and so on is not to your taste a series of push buttons could be laid out on the panel for every signal, simply needing to be pressed once to clear each signal in turn – if these are arranged to control relays in place of the track circuit relays shown here the same control could be achieved. There are few things quite as pleasing as watching the passage of the train working the signals with no input from you, however.

conjunction with lots of connections in the plugs which connect the panels to the layout. It is often cheaper and easier in this case to use relays for the control of the signals and just have one 'line wire' per signal between signal boxes which controls whether the signal will clear to yellow or green.

A simple SPDT (Single pole double throw) relay can be used; this is inexpensive, and in terms of wire and connectors saved almost works out cheaper. These 'aspect relays' are used to decide on the aspect the signal shows when it is 'off' (clear); the signal is locally controlled for the 'on' (danger) aspect, which always takes precedence (B).

Another refinement, which enables a more complete system to be developed, is the use of signal relays (C). These take the place of the signal lever switch

Exe heads up past the down advanced starter. This has no manual control, and is worked through aspect relays and a signal relay cleared by the block system when a train is on line in the right direction and reset by the track circuit just beyond it, which in this case is holding it at red. This block system is used, through indicator lights on the panels at both ends, to form the communication system between the two ends of the garden. I'm not quite sure at which stage it was that the Southern was planning on signalling the Lynton and Barnstaple with four aspect signalling, but I'm sure they would have got round to it eventually...

in the above arrangement. Once the signal relay has cleared to the off position the appropriate aspect will be decided by the aspect relays and displayed. These signal relays can then be used to extend the system to any desired level of complexity – they can either be simply arranged to work from a switch on the panel or from track circuits or the block system.

Colour light signals also often apply to multiple routes for each signal head, and consequently things like route indicators are then required. These are fairly straightforward as they are wired through contacts on relays worked by the points in the same way as a LED indicating the points on the panel. The route indicator bulbs themselves will only be illuminated when the signal is off, so a set of contacts on the signal switch or signal relay is needed to cut the supply when the signal is on. Often it is simplest to use a separate return wire in the actual signal head for the route indicator bulbs and switch the return path of the route indicators as a group to achieve this. Shunt signals are the same but opposite, only clearing with the main head at danger if on the same post.

Although this is beginning to appear horribly complicated it really isn't anything more than very simple but fairly well thought out circuits – there are just quite a few of them.

COMMUNICATION SYSTEMS

As mentioned above, signalling in the garden is a very useful way of operating a system between two stations under separate control to ensure they are in accord over who will send the other a train and when. If two stations on a system are situated one in a garage and one in the garden, or far enough apart to make shouting between them impractical or annoying, some form of electrical indication of the state of the line between stations is

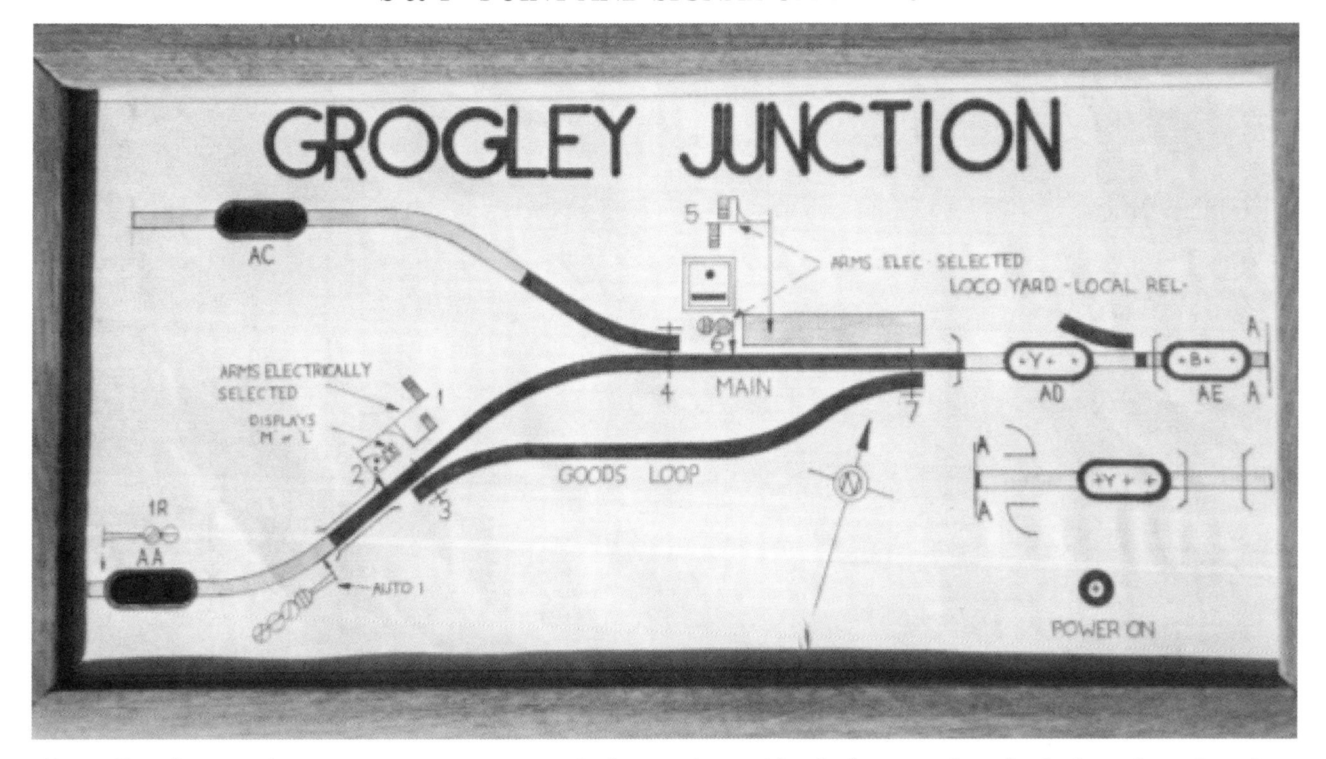

A signalling diagram drawn to prototype practice, which not only provides the lever numbers for the lever frame but also provides an indication of which track circuits are occupied, the red lozenges lighting up when a train is sat on the section of line indicated

necessary. Some form of communication is also needed to request permission to send a train and so on. The prototype system of bells and block instruments is well known and if prototype equipment can be used this is easiest, but block instruments have a high collectable value and are few and far between these days. There are other options available.

A simple form of communication can be worked from the distant and advanced starter of two respective stations by repeating their indications in the other 'box. When someone wants to send a train they set the route and pull off the advanced starting signal, at which point the next box, seeing the advance come off, can anticipate the train, set a route, and pull the signals (distant last) at which point the first box knows they can send the train. An 'accept' light could be used instead of a distant – this is a fairly similar system to the tokenless block system developed by BR and used on secondary single track lines like the Salisbury-Exeter line. This system replaces the need for physical handing over of a token, which entails slowing to 15mph, by having an electrical system which basically does the same thing ensuring only one train can occupy a section at once. This is achieved by wiring the block system with the signal circuits so that a train can only pass a starter or advanced starter on to a single line if the block ahead is clear and any oncoming signals are at danger.

There are many options available to enable communication between adjacent operating positions, and whole books could be written on the subject. Suffice here to say, a working signalling system makes it very much easier to anticipate what the other operators are trying to do.

TRACK CIRCUITS

Out in the garden, when trains are quite often out of sight of the operator, an indication of where on earth they have got to can be very useful – especially in the case of a set of points being somehow out of sight, in which case the operator needs to know where the train has got to and when they can change the points. With an indication of where the trains are comes the ability to work signals by the passage of the trains, to automatically isolate them at the end of sidings, to reverse them automatically in appropriate places – in short, some form of train detection really comes into its own outside.

I favour electronic track circuits which replicate the continuous detection of the real thing over all other options, mainly because they work with anyone's stock, which is a definite advantage in the garden where you often run a friend's stock which is unlikely to be fitted with magnets to operate reed switches or the like. Electronic track circuits also give an indication of whether or not the loco is actually drawing current, which is the most useful piece of information when it's running towards you out of sight – if it stops being detected it has either derailed or stalled or got stuck on something, and you know you need to go and investigate.

Personally I use the EDOTIS units as described in Roger Amos's book, "Practical Electronics for the Railway Modeller." I run these off a nine volt battery and take the output through a reed relay which switches on the relatively large current when a small current flows in the detection circuit, avoiding draining the batteries quickly by asking them to work the track circuit relays.

These units took a bit of getting used to, I would have to confess, but I would say persevere, as watching a train thundering round the garden returning signals to red as it passes them, and the signals then stepping back up automatically once it has passed is quite simply a joy to behold. I have now graduated to using the circuit in the second edition of the book, which uses less transistors although I still use the 2N3055 transistors of the older circuit, and I can also build this circuit on a tagboard whereas the older EDOTIS units required PCBs to hold the components. They do give out a lower output of only about a volt however, which is a bit of a disadvantage - a slight re-arrangement with an extra resistor and this can be increased to five volts which I run through the aforementioned reed relay, which in turn operates the track circuit relay, and that the signal relays, block release relays, track circuit locking relays and any of the other prototype circuits I have tried to emulate.

One point to remember is that these units don't like rain, if they play up after a wet spell it's because of the current seeping between the rails through the ballast and giving a 'false occupied' indication. This happens occasionally on the real thing too, with long track circuits in damp cuttings, and the only remedy is just to wait for it to dry out.

The evolution of a design for a building in the garden. From the photo taken on holiday in France the sketch is drawn up, first in pencil, until it looks about right and then inked in and some rough measurements sorted out to build the actual model building to. This little building stands at the end of the loop at Aixe-sur-Vienne station in the Limousin, I'm not entirely sure what it was for in reality but it was perfect for covering the point motors for my loco yard!

8

CREATING THE BUILT ENVIRONMENT

Most garden railway builders I have known have either over time built, or would like to build if they could get planning permission from the domestic department, some of the buildings so integral to the prototype railway scene - the platforms for the trains to stop at, the small retaining walls, culverts and other small infrastructure features which go to make up the railway scene. A station building, signal box and goods shed quickly turn a fairly boring collection of track on a piece of wood into a three dimensional railway, giving much more interesting and believable viewpoints and photo opportunities for the trains running on the layout. Platforms can also be built, level crossings installed and any number of other prototypical features added to bring the railway to life. This section details ways of constructing these features which can bring so much more enjoyment to a garden railway.

BUILDINGS

There are a few basic ways in which buildings can be constructed in the garden. The most important feature of these buildings is that they have to be able to withstand the weather, which can be, as I hope I have managed to convince you, a very destructive force. While wood makes an excellent medium for the base of buildings destined to spend their life on a layout inside, it is no good at all after a couple of years outside unless you are using incredibly expensive hardwood. Plasticard is an option for smaller buildings – relay cabinets to house point motors or small signal boxes are good examples – but it is not ideal, going brittle over time and being difficult to join together in a truly weatherproof way. My preferred building material is mortar as few things are more weather resistant and it looks the part entirely, but there are inherent problems with it – it's time consuming to construct and isn't really suitable for smaller buildings due to the necessary thickness of the walls.

This section details the basic construction process for these two main different types of building – those from plasticard and those from cement. Hopefully the advantages and pitfalls of each approach will become apparent as they are described. The same techniques are used to construct other forms of infrastructure such as small retaining walls – I use exactly the same process for wall construction as that described below for buildings.

There are a few general points which apply to all types of buildings. The first one is the design process for the buildings themselves. Whereas inside a building might result from weeks of detailed research and a site visit shooting reels of film and taking reams of measurements, in the garden this would be fairly pointless as you won't be

What a shame I didn't quite get round to finishing the building once I had started it – I think the excuse was that I had to attach something to the tops of the wires poking out of the walls for the light, but that would hardly have killed me. The half finished engine shed does, however, demonstrate the construction of such buildings well.

able to represent any of the detail you observe in a way which will withstand the weather. Much more important than every stone being in the right place for a building in the garden is that it looks right from a distance, so that in broad terms, it looks the part, bearing in mind that normal viewing distance in the garden could be 20 feet or so for a grown man looking at a building on the ground. What is critical is that the windows are about the right size, the panes in the right proportions and the overall dimensions of the structure in keeping with the size of window used. The easiest way to sort all this out, I find, is to begin by sketching a building and from this honing down the dimensions required for it, by all means working from a photo of a prototypical building.

The other general lesson worth learning is that buildings can look particularly silly abandoned half way through the construction process. I build up cement walls layer by layer, and usually something more interesting distracts me half way through a building, leaving shells with a few windows and no roofs dotted round the garden. The accompanying illustration depicts this point. Regardless of the presence of the 08, the eye is drawn to the incomplete engine shed which looks like it should be in war torn Warsaw on the left. The same could be said for what will eventually be a chapel in the background – only after I had taken most of the photos for this book on the stretch of line behind it did I eventually get round to building the bell tower which, looking at the photos, I now regret.

Apart from those two concepts, making buildings for the garden is more or less a case of just doing what seems like common sense.

BUILDINGS FROM PLASTICARD

Plasticard is, as inside, a good material to build small buildings from. Its failings lie in the way it deals with the weather – moderately is about the best which could be said for it, but by being careful you can make sure that this is sufficient. You have to remember to build the joints up with thick fillets of plasticard on the inside – 100 thou square as a minimum - otherwise the solvent glue simply doesn't get enough grip. All the glues I have tried go brittle over time – the more aggressive the initial bond, the quicker it snaps in the frost. I tend to use Humbrol liquid poly now which is the best I have come across and if a joint breaks outside I stick it back together with Evostick. I tend not to use this straight off because of its rather aggressive nature and the fact it often melts and distorts the plastic, but if you have a building which simply has to stay in one waterproof piece (protecting a critical point detection switch, for example) I would recommend sticking the corners together with Evostick from the outset.

There is no real difference between building plasticard buildings outside to inside – the techniques are exactly the same and well documented elsewhere. The important thing to bear in mind is the fact the building needs to deal with the weather. If you find yourself getting

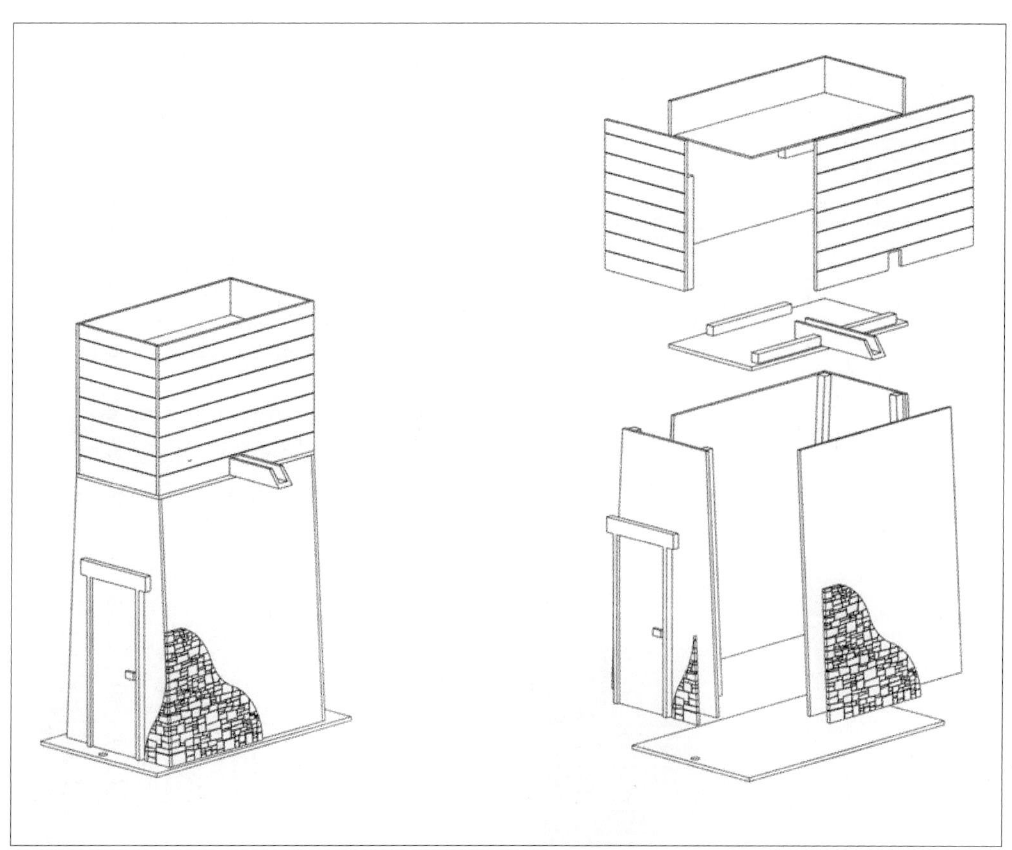

This drawing demonstrates the approach I would use to construct a small structure such as this watertower from styrene sheet in the garden. Significant reinforcement to every joint, increasing the area the solvent glue has to act over, is the key to success. The method of fixing the base has been left off this drawing - I would either, for a permanent structure, use 100 thou strip to reinforce the connection to the base or I would use some inch high walls inside the tower to locate the structure over a point motor and allow removal for maintenance.

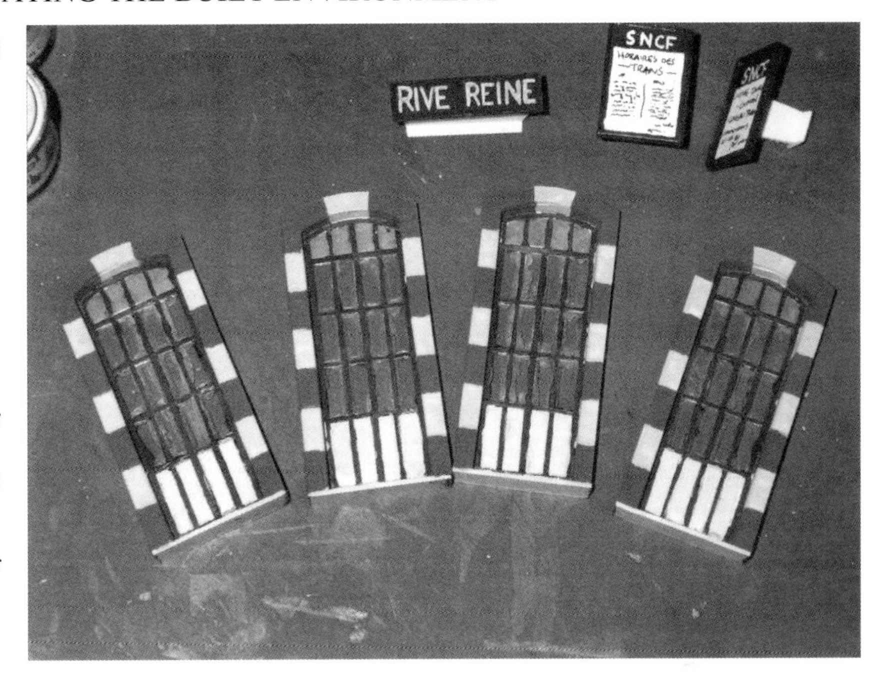

The various component parts (less roof) of a building, in this case Rive Reine station building, before installation. The windows are more or less to the standard pattern mentioned below in plasticard, and the other details fabricated from the same material – to stick them rigidly in the walls you need to attach something behind them to actually build into the mortar of the walls. I have used off-cuts of spare plasticard beam sections here, which are perfect – this is easiest to see on the notice board on the right. The rear flange stops the details falling forwards out of the wall and the web makes sure they are anchored deep into the building. The writing is just waterproof drawing pen on white paint – this lasts a surprisingly long time outside.

carried away detailing something, hold back, because you'll hardly be able to see it outside and anyway, over time, the weather will wreck anything too small.

When making small buildings to cover point motors and so on, it is of course desirable to make a portion of them removable to allow access for maintenance. It seems most obvious to do this by making the roof removable, however these small roofs tend to be rather susceptible to being blown around the garden on the wind – I find it works better to build the walls and roof as one unit and split the building around the base, a short upstand inside the walls at the bottom holding the building in situ.

When it comes to painting plasticard buildings, or in fact anything outside really, it's important that decent paint is used and that it sticks well, as the weather seems to eat away at painted models in the garden with the same appetite that it eats away at window bars in reality. I use oil paints virtually exclusively, roughening the surface of any plasticard with sandpaper to get a really good 'key' for the paint, and cleaning and priming metal with self-etch primer. Painted like this, the finish will last a good few winters before it requires sprucing up again with another coat, just like the real thing.

BUILDINGS FROM CEMENT

Building from cement is, as I mentioned above, by far my preferred method of construction. I build the roofs, windows, doors etc out of plasticard along similar lines to those described above, and then the walls are built up a bit at a time to create the shell of the building.

The first step is to cast a base slab in place, which doesn't have to be huge in scale – I generally make them a couple of inches thick and cast them in situ where the building will eventually stand. If it is intended to have a working light in the building remember to cast some wires in through the base at this stage, although it can be drilled later it's a lot easier to get it right now! I build up the first inch or so of the walls as an integral part of the base, so

Using both trowel and spare hand to mix mortar on a board, in this case for a building. Mortar for buildings needs to be quite dry so it will stand – a lot less water is used than for its bricklaying counterpart

Pulling the wet mortar down over the already dried section built up before with my thumb (on the right). This ensures a good bond, and needs to be done with reasonable force. As a general note, be careful about getting too much cement on your hands – obviously some is unavoidable, but wash your hands reasonably soon after handling it as it is strongly alkaline when wet, which isn't good for the skin.

Up to first floor level. The bits of slate are for what become external walls at a higher level. You can clearly imagine the benefit of a bit of beam on the back of the station nameboard here, once it's built in it'll never come out again.

any doors or floor-to ceiling windows will need to be included at this stage.

I tend to paint the plasticard parts first and then install them to avoid getting paint all over the concrete, but you do have to be careful not to have cement on your fingers and smear it all over the paint which also marks badly. I use a different mix for all buildings to bricklaying – three parts of sharp sand (for texture) to one of building sand (for strength and some colouring) to one of cement. Four parts to one part is quite strong, but the buildings need the strength in their thin walls.

I mix this on a board generally – the easiest way is as shown, using the trowel and the other hand together to speedily mix the constituents. The water content of this mix is completely different to that for, say, laying bricks. Here you need a fairly stiff mix to stand upright whereas bricklaying mortar would just fall over – careful control of the water when mixing and using a splash of washing up liquid should stop any disastrously sloppy mixes. If is does all get a bit wet add some more sand and cement – if you end up putting loads in try and keep it roughly in proportion, but don't worry too much about this – if the proportions of various mixes vary slightly you just end up with some nice variation in mix up the wall, as so often seen in reality.

The walls are then built up slowly, an inch or two at a time, which is about all that will stand wet. Often, as with pointing brickwork, I build the wall up and then come back an hour later when it has dried out a bit to shape it with a trowel – particularly to get nice sharp corners. To get a rough finish to the concrete you have to use your fingers to build up the cement a little bit at a time. This looks so much more realistic once finished than the result from casting the walls against something, which will give a smooth finish. To get the first wet mortar to stick on to the dry mortar further down the wall you have to squash it on quite hard and then 'tease' it down over the edges of the wall, this gives quite a reasonably strong joint as long as you do it with a degree of firmness.

As you build up the walls you will, of course, need to include the windows. Through building a fair few of these I have come to develop the design shown opposite as easiest, quickest and most robust. For years I stuck glazing bars on as I would inside – I have now given up on that as far too much work for no reward outside, and use a tippex pen to paint the glazing bars on the back of the glazing material. I used to use thin plastic sheet, which is fine but thicker acrylic is more robust – I prefer the two millimetres thick variety which can be culled from plastic clip frames or similar, which accepts solvent well enough and, more importantly, is thick enough to avoid warping in

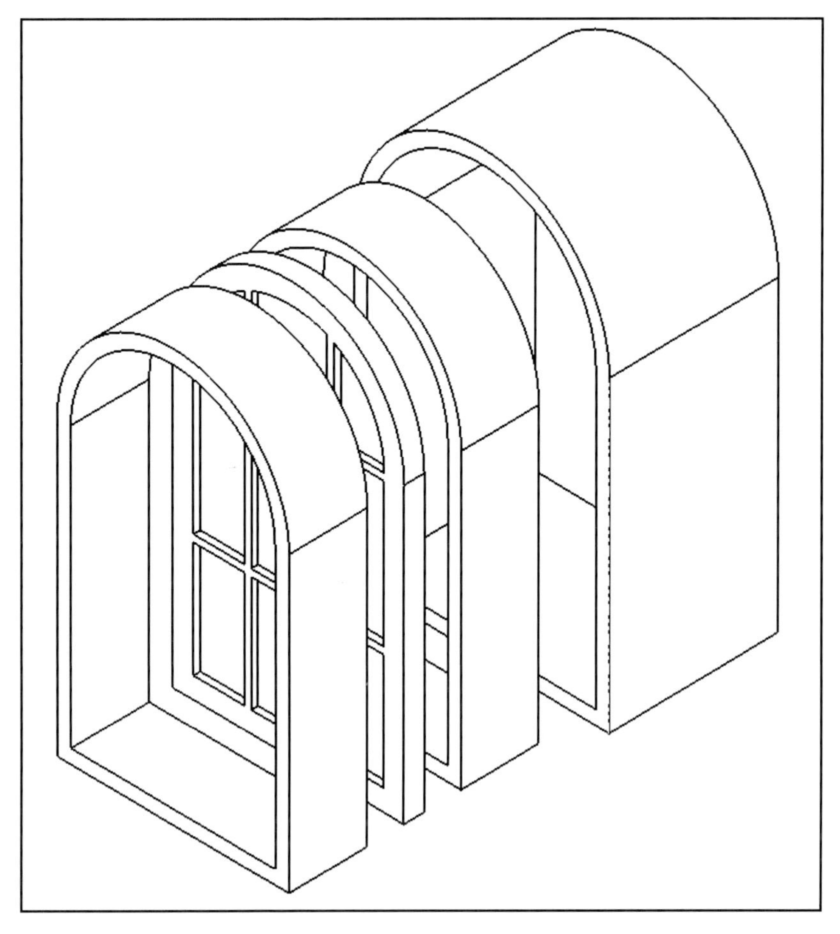

The standard window unit I use, built up out of plasticard. The actual glazing, with the bars painted on, is sandwiched between the two half – depth frames, out of 40 thou plasticard or similar, and these are glued inside the outer shell. The resulting window is solid, weatherproof, quick to build and looks the part.

the weather. This glazing sheet is sandwiched in the window 'frame' – I had a lot of trouble with early windows getting pushed into the buildings as there was nothing to restrain them once the glue had given up the ghost. I now make three 'frames' – an outer one, usually in 40 thou or so, which is the full depth of the wall and then two which are half the depth and fit inside this outer shell, between which the glazing is sandwiched. To get the curve shown at the top I bend the plasticard round a piece of wood and then immerse it in boiling water. Rectangular windows are, of course, somewhat easier to build up.

Once the roof level is reached you need to level off the top of the building, at least roughly. This is easiest, I find, with a big building trowel. Once you know the pitch of the roof you can actually construct it – it is not worth trying to jump the gun on this one, I find. If you try building the roof at the outset and then adjusting the building to fit it never quite does.

ROOFS

I build roofs out of plasticard – 40 thou at least - with all joints held together with at least a 100 thou square batten down the inside to give the glue a decent area to stick on, following the principles of plasticard building construction outlined above. Slates I usually represent with plasticard embossed to represent paving slabs – I can never quite be bothered to buy the slate sheets and cut them into strips, sticking them all on individually outside as I would inside. You need a glue which you can spread out over the whole area of the roof before it dries as solvent glues would evaporate far too fast, I tend to revert to good old polystyrene cement in a tube.

I then spray the roofs with plastic grey primer, mix a bit of black spray paint in for colour variation and paint the bargeboards, ending up with a roof as shown overleaf. If I am not going to need to get into the building in a hurry then I stick the entire roof on top of the walls with silicone sealant which takes up the slack in the walls but could easily be cut out were I to have to get into the building to change a bulb or similar. Sometimes roofs have to be removable, for example on an engine shed so you can clean the track inside – in this case I hang a large plumbing fitting underneath to stop the wind taking it off into orbit.

PLATFORMS

I have, I fear, yet to find the ideal way to construct platforms for garden railways. In the past I have used budgie grit sprinkled on wet cement to give a realistic surface, but while this looks excellent for a short while after a year or two the budgie grit starts migrating and getting stuck in turnouts and all manner of other places it would be decidedly better were it not. When I next build a

The stages in station platform construction are all shown in this view of the new island platform at the bottom of the garden. The rammed hardcore bed, visible in the foreground, has been blinded off here with some old sand - this is not essential but limits the amount of mortar required, and I nearly always seem to have a pile of less-than-perfect sand in a corner somewhere that has been swept up after concrete mixing or some similarly messy activity. The hole left for the station lights, cabling already installed, is visible towards the top of the photo.

platform I intend to mix a very fine form of concrete with this budgie grit and lay that on the surface of the platform in an attempt to bond it in better rather than to rely on the weak cement - aggregate bond.

When building platforms, again remember to put in wires for the lights if you intend to make them work (which I recommend) – it would be very difficult to come back afterwards and install them, and also bear in mind that the platforms need to be fairly solid as inevitably, sooner or later, something heavy will get put on them – usually you standing on them to try to reach a loco reluctant to move over a sticky set of points. They also have to cope with ground movement in the same way as the walls carrying the track, so similarly, don't skimp on a decent base.

I build platforms up starting with the walling along the edge, which is cement cast around a bit of old wire to stop it breaking up, this wire being set out first with the aid of a long coach to make sure its position caters for the requirements of end and centre throw, where the middle of the coach moves out over the inside rail as it travels around a curve. I generally wrap the wire around nails hammered into the trackbase for alignment.

Between these two walls, once they have dried, I prepare a really good solid base of rammed hardcore, which is an essential requirement to prevent movement over time, and cast an inch or two of mortar (the usual 3:1:1 mix of sharp sand : building sand : cement) over this. I then wet the surface with a watering can and sprinkle the budgie grit where it is required. After a few weeks I vacuum off any surplus. The discolouration to the track visible in the photo is best dealt with by washing the cement off as soon as practical with a watering can full of water, otherwise it will stain.

If the platforms are for a standard gauge line with the trains running between the platform faces then they can be cast against a formwork or a plastic platform face can be used such as the Peco product. I have no experience of these but I'm sure they would work as well as their track outside. Plasticard platforms are, of course, possible, but beware of what the heat will do to distort such a large area of plastic under the midday sun. To be honest, they are nothing like as durable as concrete ones.

The various portions of roof for the French station building. These are all constructed from 40 thou plasticard with paving slab embossed plasticard overlaid to mimic slates

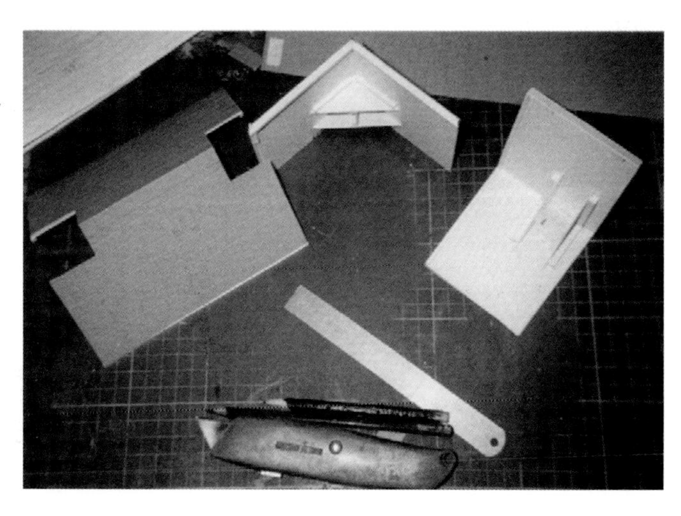

9

THE FINISHING TOUCHES

There is a certain magical quality to garden railways and miniature landscapes which are lit at night. All manner of people - young and old, the railway loving and the downright uninitiated appear fascinated by the lights and rush about the garden in an effort to see them all and point them out to each other. It isn't very difficult to arrange a few lights, and I cannot urge you strongly enough to consider doing so when building a railway in the garden. Linking them all up is something which 'can follow' in much the same way as most other things when the initial push to get the trains running is taking place, but it's not very complicated and the result well repays the effort involved. The lights on my line are all wired on a 'lighting ring main' which goes right round the garden, linking up the lights on the way, and while it can be fed through either panel when the railway is working it can also be fed through a switch permanently wired up in the hut, so come a winter's night when the trains aren't running I can still just switch the power on inside and all the lights come on for the benefit and enjoyment of parting guests without requiring me to find, dust off and plug in control panels in the dark.

LIGHTING THE RAILWAY

The challenge in lighting garden railways lies in finding ways and places to position bulbs to create the desired impression of a believable miniature landscape at night and capture the magic which these small bulbs can create. Bright, constant lighting for a busy station can be arranged as easily as the dim flicker of a single oil lamp on an isolated halt or the lonely yellow glow of a far flung distant signal, and thought needs to be applied to giving the right effect in the right places. The beauty of the garden is that it allows space between stations, which becomes almost magnified at night, with clustered pools of light at stations separated by a lot of darkness. This gives a real sense of travelling between stations, and it is as important to maintain these dark spaces as to light the others. If you are running trains complete with internal lights the effect is magnified yet further by watching the train snaking its way around the landscape, heading for a distant pool of light signalling the next station. There are three main 'types' of lighting – illuminated buildings, individual lamp standards and signal lights. The signals have been dealt with separately in the signalling section, suffice to say here that I wire the bulbs in the actual semaphore signals up with a diode between the 'signalling' supply line, from which they are normally fed, and the 'lighting ring main' which runs round the garden, so if the garden lights are turned on without the trains running the signal lamps will still light up.

BUILDING LIGHTING

Buildings can be lit by any form of bulb – I tend to use a grain of wheat bulb. This is just fixed inside a building as it is finished, the wires having been cast in the

Rolling into Grogley Junction just as darkness falls, the station lamps reflect off the railheads as we swing into the loop. The advantage of building a grain of wheat bulb into the signal lamps is clearly shown. This photo was taken as it was getting dusky - the effect is greatly enhanced when it's actually dark, but a bit difficult to photograph. In this instance, the garden lights have been turned on from inside using the 'lighting ring main' discussed in the text. A diode between that and the signalling feed which normally supplies all the signal lights (and a few other signalling functions) powers the signal lamps when I just want to turn the lights on without connecting the control panels up. Failing to connect up the control panels does of course mean the line isn't interlocked, however - and some very special combinations of signalled route and turnout setting can be accidentally created.

A single grain of wheat bulb illuminates the inside of the engine shed at Rive Reine on a somewhat chilly night - an example of 'less-is-more' building illumination. This is also another example of using the 'Lighting Ring Main' - running trains in such conditions would not be advisable!

floor slab back at the beginning of the building's construction. I tend to glue the roofs on buildings to stop them blowing round in the wind, but I very rarely experience problems with bulbs in buildings and have never found sticking the roofs on a problem. If a bulb does fail I drill a small (6mm) hole through the building in some inconspicuous place and 'post' another grain of wheat bulb in. This technique also works well when you inadvertently forget to cast the wires in the floor slab.

A lamp in the middle of a building shell will, obviously, show through all the windows – if a more accurate approach is desired, with only some windows lit, the easiest thing to do is to create 'light boxes' behind the windows. To do this I use some sheet metal culled from something like an old biscuit tin or baking tray - plasticard will melt - built in as the walls go up. Some form of ventilation into a common roof space or similar is desirable to avoid excessive overheating – filament bulbs get hot. An alternative now available is, of course, the white LED. These give a very hard bluish-white light however; to get a more realistic gas lamp effect either use a high resistance, or paint them with a thinned down wash of translucent yellow paint.

Adding exterior lights to a building, such as a lamp over a porch, can be very atmospheric – these are built in exactly the same way as the standard lamps below, just remember to poke some wires through the walls as you build them.

STANDARD LAMPS

These most commonly take the guise of station lamps, although streetlights or yard lamps are equally effective. They can either be bought – often as whitemetal castings – or fabricated. I have always fabricated them from brass around a grain of wheat bulb, although this would be more complicated in a scale smaller than 7mm scale. Brass lamps are slightly more likely to withstand knocks and bumps outside than their whitemetal counterparts, but they are far from immune, and for some reason wherever placed they seem to attract errant sleeves when track cleaning or sweeping a piece of debris from the line. The illustration opposite shows the construction of the generic freelance lamps I have built for the French-influenced station on my garden railway, based very loosely on an SNCF design. The grain of wheat bulbs are easily obtainable, the brass tube for the supports is available from most DIY stores which sell it in longer, cheaper lengths than those usually available in the modelling trade, and the reflectors are standard buttons turned upside down - I think the poor lady in the fabric shop was a bit confused by the importance I was placing on the shape of the back of the button!

The details can, of course, be changed to suit a particular railway company – my other station is equipped with lamps based on the Southern Railway design at Lynton with the characteristic swan neck, again fabricated from brass. The wiring for the lamps is cast into the

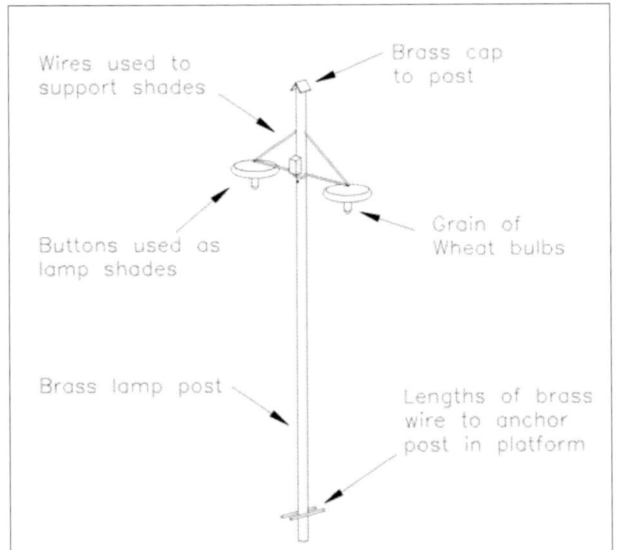

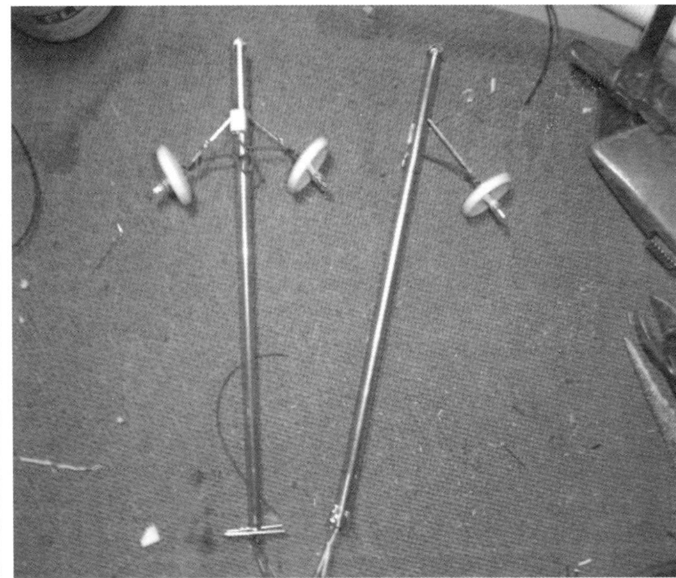

In the garden prototypically sized platforms means significantly more of details such as station lamps and station name boards are required than would be the case for a layout built inside. An approach to their construction therefore needs to be developed which is both robust and easily reproducible. This drawing and the accompanying photograph demonstrate this process of simplification and rationalisation, detailing the method used to construct the station lights which are representative of an SNCF design.

platform, as shown in section 8 above, as are the bottoms of the lamps themselves once they are installed.

Lamps on the corner of buildings or high on walls are often used in reality to light an area where the public will walk – these are just as effective in model form as in real life, casting a pool of light on the ground below them. I would suggest fabrication in brass as above.

LIGHTING THE GARDEN

If the railway more closely resembles a test track in the garden rather than a landscape in miniature it could be more appropriate to light the garden as opposed to lighting the railway. This is easily accomplished by using some of the large range of garden lights available - a quick trip to a DIY store will demonstrate just how great the range of products for this market now is. If the line runs close to a building, standard halogen floodlights can be screwed on the wall – the possibilities are virtually endless. It can be useful to have a large floodlight like this to turn on after an operating session to make sure you've picked everything up – certainly I find the one on the end of our garage particularly useful to check no wagons have been forgotten in the end of one of the many sidings and loops hidden in dark corners of our garden when clearing up after an operating session that has lasted on into the night.

If water features are incorporated into the line, it is worth lighting these, too – a waterfall with a couple of blue lights in it is a fascinating, magical thing to watch after dark, enthralling most people who see it. I used a couple of MES bulbs (the small screw-in bulbs commonly available) initially to illuminate mine with stage lighting gel wrapped around them, but there are a number of more professional products on the market which could be used.

A large number of the garden lights available run off a 24v dedicated supply – I would recommend just wiring the lighting through this system separately to the railway, as 24 volts is not a very useful voltage for garden railway electrics and is likely to severely damage relays, signals or trains if you accidentally connect it up to the wrong thing.

WATER FEATURES IN THE GARDEN

Running water has always fascinated me, and it has, in my opinion, greatly enhanced the gardens I have known which have employed it. A twelve coach train streaking over a river bridge, the water running swiftly underneath is a sight to behold, and well worth the actually fairly minimal amount of effort required to get the water moving. This book does not intend to explain how to build a pond – there are plenty of other books on the subject, but small scale water features are fairly specific to model railways in the garden, and an approach to their construction is explained below.

THE PUMP

If you want water to move you're going to need a pump to move it. There are many pond pumps on the market, both for working off mains and off a low voltage supply, and any of them is suitable for operating around a model railway – just follow the maker's instructions. For smaller water systems - a waterwheel for example, or a small waterfall - a smaller pump can be used. I have found the little 12 volt pumps designed for use in caravans particularly effective, pumping an impressive flow of water and working off a useful voltage – I run mine off a 12 volt battery charger. They're not continuously rated, meaning you have to turn them off every now and again to let them cool down, but that's far from the end of the world.

If you are going to install a non-standard pump you are going to need to build a sump for it to work in, but this is easily achieved. You can of course just use the pond as a sump, and I did just that for a while, but the water gets full of muck which, eventually, seems to get itself stuck in the end of the pump, dramatically reducing its effectiveness. I now use a separate sump made from a length of four inch soil pipe with a standard bung in the end from a plumbing fittings shop. This makes for a completely waterproof sump. You need quite a large capacity, sufficient to absorb all the water out of the system as it drains back down to the bottom when you switch the pump off – this can require a relatively deep hole, but that's not really a problem to dig – we are, after all, in the serious business of constructing railways here. As with foundations, just get stuck in with some decent tools.

Once the sump has been built, the pump can be installed at the bottom on the end of a piece of hose. A filter should be cut from a piece of foam (from an upholsterer's shop) to sit above the pump to intercept the worst of the muck which ends up going round the system. At the top of the rising main a tee piece and valve should be installed to allow a degree of recirculation.

The sump lid is cast from concrete in situ to get a close fitting shape to prevent any slugs and snails getting in it - they just love to live in sumps, and more to the point, die in them, making the whole place less than pleasant.

To form the lid first cast the outside around the top of the soil pipe to provide a haunch and also retain the soil at the top. Then avoid the temptation to do more and come back the day after to cast the lid itself. I cast this against a bit of a plastic bag to stop it sticking to the support below, and held the concrete up with several layers of cardboard cut to roughly the right size resting on the pipes underneath. A bit of old wire is pushed in to make a handle and the whole left for a few days before it is disturbed. Once you have stripped out the 'formwork' you are left with an accurately shaped, snugly fitting lid to your sump.

A float switch is quite a good idea to control the electrical feed to the pump and stop it running dry when the level of the water drops, which will quickly wreck the pump, as when devoid of water it will run at a much higher speed and quickly heat up. Either a microswitch with a bit of rail soldered on the end of the operating arm and a film pot strapped to the end to act as a float, as I had for quite some time, or a proprietary switch can be used – the proprietary ones are more expensive but take up less space. They need to be mounted somehow so that the float can be pushed up to allow current to flow to the pump when the water level is sufficiently high to allow the pump to run without danger of it running dry.

WATERWHEELS AND WATERFALLS

The actual waterwheel and headrace are from plasticard, the wheel pivoting on a brass axle. It doesn't work anything in the way of flat rods, despite my great schemes – I don't think it would have the strength to, but it looks good going round, and the movement and the sound from it really add something interesting to focus on between the trains.

The rest of the channels and so on are from cement - the standard 3:1:1 mix of sharp sand : building sand : cement that I use for most things. The key is to make them fairly thick below ground, a good three inches or so, to allow them to deal with ground movement, or the odd knock.

Waterfalls I build out of slate - I brought a great lump from a garden centre several years ago, and I'm still splitting bits off it now. There is nothing difficult to their construction, just try to make them look as natural as possible, and with plenty of opportunity for overhanging plants to grow down into the water.

PLANTS AND GREENERY

The garden railway seems like the ideal place to diversify into 'live landscaping' as I have heard it described, carefully trimming box hedges around the line to represent the landscape beyond the company fence. This is a subject I have to confess to knowing little about – no plants really scale well against a railway built to less than 10mm: foot or so and the area of planting around garden railways is much better explained by someone with experience in SM32 or G45, to which end I would point you to Tag Gorton's excellent book should you wish to explore the possibilities in this area. My experiments stretch to a few miniature conifers which aren't so miniature four years on and a couple of heather plants, which I am quite pleased with despite the fact the bigger scale boys recommend against them. They may well not really represent any kind of scale plant, but then in 'O' gauge nothing really does, and a heather plant at least hides the wiring beside the railway and conveniently shields the point motor at the end of the loop.

Walls with railways on top can be greatly enhanced by some careful and more conventional planting, which blends the wall into the garden and can make getting planning permission from the domestic department considerably easier.

10

STOCK AND OPERATION

The trains to actually run on a garden railway are, really, no different from those which run on their inside counterparts. In the case of a test track in the garden kind of railway there is no difference, the trains just being run in on the garden line. When a system is being built up from scratch in the garden the stock can be built specifically for it, and in this case a few differences in the constructional approach can be employed.

Whereas for inside model railways it always seems that model locomotives should almost be rivet-perfect, in the garden this is far less important and you can be much less exacting in your standards. More important outside is that the impression formed by the model is right – that the shape of the chimney and the dome and the overall proportions of the model don't jar the eye - details such as the number of spokes in the driving wheels or the exact type of lubricator used are far less important because, at garden viewing distances, you just won't be able to see them.

The same applies to the stock – the great thing about garden railways is the length of trains which can be run, and the impression formed by 72 loaded coal wagons rumbling by behind a grubby 8F is so striking no-one will ever notice if they are all running with the same wagon number, or that they are straight out of the Hornby catalogue. Of course, having said all that, I still strive to build detailed models to run outside because I like to think that they look good on the shelf inside too, but the point is

The last train of the day rattles down the grade behind the 08. Running rakes like this round the garden are what summer days are all about.

A couple of wagons from Peco kits rest in what is supposed to be the catch point out of the engine sheds - but then I don't really have enough sidings! A different paint job can make all the difference in the garden between two wagons which are actually the same, and I would wholeheartedly recommend taking advantage of this fact and using lots of kit based wagons to save time building them from scratch so you can get on with the really important business of running trains. The covered wagon is exactly the same kit as the Lynton and Barnstaple wagons which appear elsewhere in these pages, but you'd hardly notice the similarity out here.

that this is not essential in the garden, and the sight of 12 very old ready to run coaches running behind an equally old and, to be honest, inaccurate Britannia looks as good as a supremely detailed B4 tank with three ballast wagons and a break van waiting in a goods loop for a pathway down the main line.

The garden is a place where batch producing stock really comes into its own too, making one small coal wagon and getting the rest cast in resin to form a long rake. I batch build coaches to try to speed up the process.

OPERATING A GARDEN RAILWAY

In some respects operating a garden railway is just the same as operating an inside line, but the fact it is outside and subsequently influenced by the weather does make a difference. The 'garden railway season', when it is practical and enjoyable to run a garden railway, lies mostly in the summer months. While there are no hard and fast rules, it is generally a bit cold to make being outside enjoyable from about October to March, although once the daffodils start poking up and the days start getting longer I generally can't wait to get outside and start building something.

It's also a bit damp during the winter, not only making it unpleasant kneeling on the ground, but also dampness between the sleepers can create problems with voltage drop in long sections with relatively narrow gauges (up to about 00), the trains getting slower and slower. It can also completely confuse electronic track circuits, should you use them! Having said all that, I often end up trying to run some trains on Christmas Day to fill in that bit of time between the morning present session and lunch, and it would be by no means impossible to run trains the year round, should you be sufficiently hardy, or sufficiently lucky enough to have the stations and

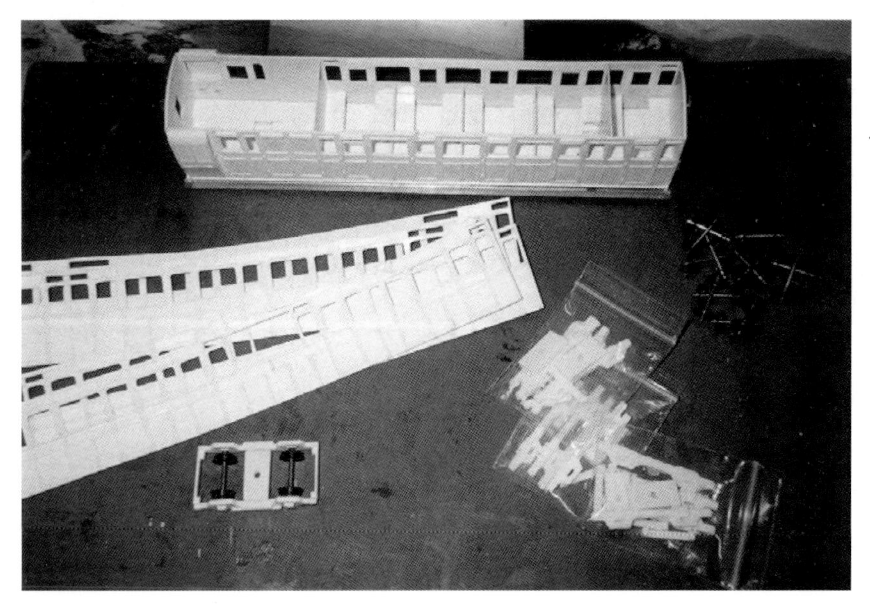

Batch building coaches for the garden. The sides, from plasticard, make excellent holiday modelling projects I find – these were built on a kitchen table in Brittany. The bogies are cast in resin to my pattern by Port Wynnstay Models, which speeds up construction , and at a very reasonable price. Building stock like this, you quickly build up to the size of train you really need to exploit the potential of garden railways.

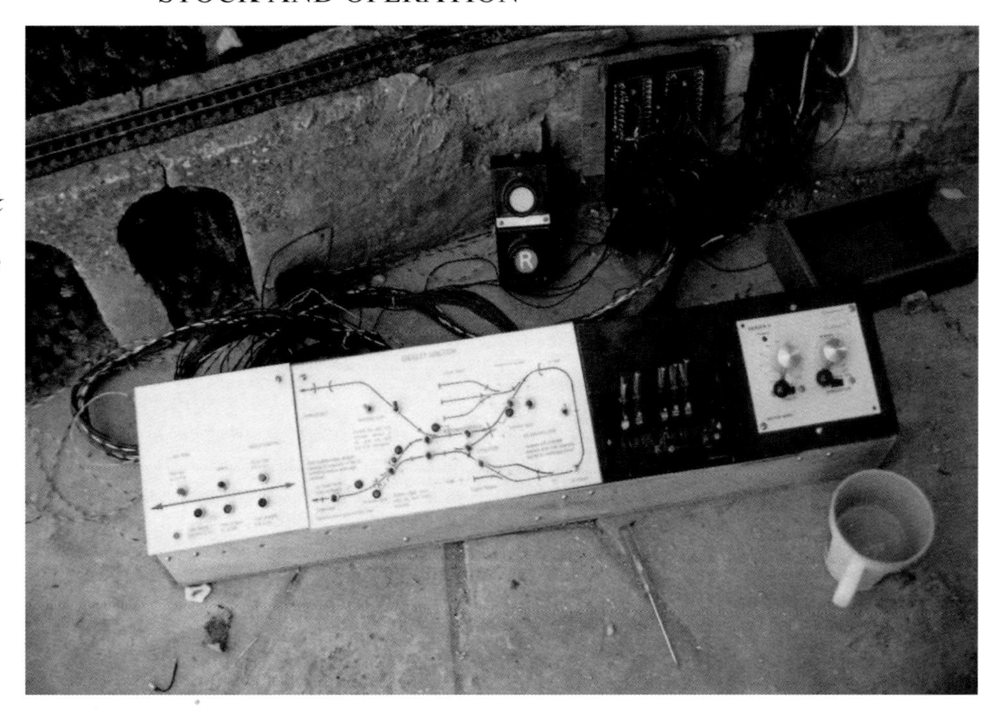

The control panel at Grogley Junction all ready for a day's operation – a cup of tea on hand, a screwdriver for uncoupling – all that's missing is a track cleaning block, which really can't be that far away – they usually seem to end up sat on the platforms, for some reason.

operating positions inside.

During the winter, if the line is not being regularly used, it is worth keeping the points moving and oiled so they work come the spring – they need just a squirt of WD40 in the point motor and a drop of electrolube on the centre-over spring and to then be changed a few times. It's never that tempting, sitting inside with a coach kit in December, to walk outside and do this, but it is well worth it to avoid having to start the next year changing turnouts and point motors.

Once the spring has arrived the first operating session of the year should be viewed purely as a fault finding session. On no account invite anyone on the promise of a working railway because the ravages of the winter will definitely have dropped a few track bonds off for you somewhere, and the odd fault will surface as you run the system which you will need a toolkit on hand to fix. Once you have overcome all these problems and got the railway working properly, however, I thoroughly recommend coercing a few like minded friends over to enjoy running trains for an afternoon – I think it is probably one of my favourite pastimes, taking up position at one of my stations, sitting on a bag of sand, the sun shining, the birds singing and the trains arriving in a nice constant stream on the main, the occasional short freight battling up the branch to keep things interesting.

A couple of hours running trains passes with great speed, so absorbed are you in making sure trains don't go back with the same engine on the front that they arrived with, marshalling brake vans to the right end of the trains and above all keeping a road free for the occasional through express. This is the kind of operation that requires a layout only a very few lucky people have sufficient room for inside, but which in the garden is commonplace.

In the garden, of course, track cleaning and wheel cleaning take on a whole new perspective that you would never imagine it could if you are used to inside layouts. Outside it is essential to clean the track thoroughly at the beginning of every operating session, during which I always seem to start cursing the amount of track I have under spiky bushes. It is also a good idea to keep the wheels clean on the locos as giving them a nudge to get them going again in the garden is much more difficult than inside, usually involving contorting yourself into some fantastically uncomfortable position around some plant or other. This is a small price to pay, however, for being able to run twelve coach trains at speed…

If you run trains every day for a period of time, a week in the summer for example, you can generally get away with not cleaning the track between running sessions – the rails don't get that dirty overnight. You'll soon know if you need to clean the track, the trains will falter and stall, in which case a swift application of the rail cleaning block will be required.

Usually all too soon in an operating session the sun sets, a meal time arrives or it starts raining, and there is then a mad scramble to get everything packed up. If you can run the trains into a suitably secure shed to store them this will make the task of packing up a lot easier, meaning you don't have to trek across the garden with piles of stock boxes, but only a really well built, dry shed would be suitable for storing trains in. Whereas for an inside layout it would probably be necessary to take boards down and pack up the actual layout you are, of course, spared this in the garden, needing only to take the stock and the control panels inside. The rest of the line then sinks back into its 'garden feature' role, ready for another day.

A pair of figures add an indisputably human touch of realism to this scene on a Gauge 1 garden railway, and the row of station lamps, as mentioned before in this book, really add a 3 dimensional aspect to the scene. The eye-level viewpoint and the wagons just in view on the left also conspire together to make this a very believable photo, despite the full-size house backs on the right - and the photo is a vivid example of the levels of believability and atmosphere that can be achieved in the garden.

11

CONCLUSIONS

I hope, having read all the above, you are not discouraged by the thought of building a garden railway, but rather waiting for the weather to clear up so you can burst outside and have a go. If it all appears horribly complicated, bear in mind that I have detailed by far the most involved way of getting trains running in the garden in describing how to build a garden railway outside. It would be much, much simpler to build a circuit of track, and from the most basic circles of track you can derive many of the chief pleasures of building railways outside. Once you have got that first circuit of track down, however, and have seen the first trains running outside, I am sure you will want to continue building and developing the layout in a way you never could inside. If you are looking for something more than the spare room can offer in terms of railway building potential I cannot urge you strongly enough that you look to the garden as a place to set the navvies to work. I'm sure gardens weren't invented for plants; they were invented for model railways.

There is something very believable about this photo of Anthony Delaine Smith's 00 garden railway, and you can just imagine the buffet of air as the trains pass at speed jolting the drivers ever so slightly in their seats.
I would argue that these ready-to-run models look much more realistic in their sunlit garden setting than they could shuffling about under a florescent tube inside - and credibility is, I think, added to the scene by its setting. It is very seldom that stretches of double track mainline without a station or a turnout in sight are modelled inside, yet there are so many hundreds of miles like this on the real railway.
This picture also demonstrates how electrical bonds around joints blend into obscurity - that in the foreground goes virtually unnoticed.

References and recommended reading

The books listed below I recall being of particular use when constructing my garden railway and writing this book. I have not included books that have provided inspiration or prototype details of a particular line - those will depend on individual taste and modelling interests.

Chudley, R., Greeno, R., (2006) *Building Construction Handbook*, 6th edition: Butterworth-Heinmann Ltd. ISBN 978-0750668224

This book gives one of the most comprehensive overviews of the building world I have ever found in print, and I would recommend it to anyone. There is a huge amount of value to the garden railway builder in this book.

Baden-Powell, C., (2001) *The Architect's Pocket Book*, 2nd edition: Architectural Press. ISBN 978-0750647649

This book, I have always thought, is basically my 4-year engineering degree in 286 pages. I would recommend it to anyone building anything.

Gorton, T., (1996) *Steam in Your Garden*, Atlantic Transport Publishers. ISBN 978-0906899670

This book sticks in my mind as having provided me with pages of inspiration many years ago, some of which still inspires me when outside building today. While geared towards larger scale narrow gauge garden railways there is a lot here which can be applied to smaller scale main lines.

Amos, R., (1982) *Practical Electronics for the Railway Modeller*, Patrick Stephens Ltd. ISBN 085059555

This book provides the circuit diagram for the EDOTIS track circuit I have come to use as standard and which is discussed in the text. The 1992 reprint contains a simpler circuit, which I use in a slightly amended fashion, but the fuller and more helpful description is in the 1982 book.

Clancy, J., (1982) *Site Surveying and Levelling,* Edward Arnold. ISBN 0-7131-3439-9

This detailed book will explain practical methods of surveying to whatever level of detail the garden railway builder desires.

All photos, unless otherwise credited, were taken by Graham or Christopher Hatton.

Acknowledgements

As I approach the end of the process of writing this book I am increasingly aware of the thanks I owe to a wide-ranging collection of individuals who have in some way shaped it, who have helped in its writing and without whom it would not exist today. Paying suitable and individual tribute to them all would perhaps be impossible, as thanks are almost equally due to those who have helped me in some way with the construction of the railway as to those who helped directly with the book, and those mentioned individually below by no means represent the extent of the list of names to which I am grateful. To those not singled out below, but who know they have helped me – thank you.

The book is dedicated to my parents, to whom perhaps I owe the greatest thanks – to my mother for her support and enthusiasm despite my destruction of large tracts of the garden that, as a Dean, is so beloved by her – and to my father, railwayman of thirty years, whose standard of modelling has never ceased to act as inspiration to me, and with whom discussing our shared hobby never grows old.

Thanks are also due to Kevin Robertson, my publisher, whose enthusiasm and professionalism have kept the project alive, and I hope we have produced a result of which we can both be very proud.

My sister, Bryony Hatton, has on occasion unwittingly acted as a much needed voice of reason, when for example coming across twenty pages discussing track circuit releases for garden railways laying on the study floor, and Victoria McIntosh provided valuable support as the end of the project drew near, both through late night phone calls convincing me of the worth of the thing when a deadline appeared to be looming horribly over me and through the loan of her laptop, on which I type this.

The Packridge Education I received from Mike Knights provided me with an introduction to the building world which I will always be grateful for, and many of the construction techniques described here were first learnt building land drains around his farm.

I thank also the people who have provided photos included in this book - particularly Dr Bob Buckland, Dennis Tillman and also Tony Wright of British Railway Modelling fame, who provided photographs of Michael Adamson's and Anthony Delaine Smith's garden railways, many of which are included in these pages.

Thanks are also due to the person who saved a last-minute disaster with reproducing prints - Jeff Geary - and to Drew Trenberth and Rob Thompson, whose CAD skills I have shamelessly tried to assimilate by looking over their shoulders while they worked.

Above: - In the growing Autumn gloom, the two electric locos run off the line leading down to the mine branch and rattle through Rive Reine station. As I look at this picture I can clearly imagine standing on that platform, and I want to pull my coat a little tighter around me to keep the growing cool of the evening, and keep the realisation that summer's over at bay. It's taken from exactly the same viewpoint as the second figure of Chapter1 however, which is decidedly a high summer photo, sun beating down on the platforms as I wait for the enginemen to hurry up and run round, fireman hanging out the window of the cab trying to get out of the heat within.

It is this change with the seasons and even the time of day which I think is one of the great advantages of garden railways and which almost make them easier to believe than an inside line which can take nothing from its domestic surroundings to place its season. The evening can also be taken advantage of, and I would thoroughly recommend installing station lights, signal lights and so on around a garden railway because watching both them and the pleasure people take from looking at a miniature landscape lit up at night is yet another way to derive enjoyment from the line you have built.

Previous page: - An Adams Radial rounds the curve at the top of the garden on Dennis Tillman's 'O' gauge garden railway. This unobtrusive line has been incorporated into the garden by careful planting on either side, and between the passing trains you hardly notice that there is a railway here at all. The line also takes full advantage of the natural slope of this garden - while at this end single row of bricks sits on top of a concrete foundation, creating a virtually ground-level line, the other is at a normal operating height in a purpose-built railway room.

Above: - This is the kind of train which looks at its best in the garden, a long rake of coaches with a big engine at the front battling up the grade, the route unfurling around every gentle curve of the track. You can almost feel the confidence and good old-fashioned railway pride of the man with his hand on the regulator. This stretch of track essentially just connects up the stations on my line, running between the fence and a flower bed to complete the continuous run and it could have been laid in a dead straight line parallel to the fence - but I am glad I didn't do so, and I would recommend not doing so because the gently wending track looks so much more realistic, as this photo shows. The advantage of cutting accurately shaped 'ballast' is also apparent, giving a nice neat shoulder reminiscent of the real thing. Again, out of scale sleepers go virtually unnoticed - something that would never happen inside.

For me, this photo somehow manages to capture some of the idyllic laziness of narrow gauge railways, and I can't imagine that the fireman has been dispatched to the 'box in a great hurry to find out why that signal is resolutely on. Far more likely, I would imagine, that he and the driver are just shutting the injector steam valves having topped up the boiler to keep it quiet for a while, and are about to wipe the cab seats down with a bundle of cotton waste before sitting down and discussing the merits of this new-fangled Southern Railway, waiting for the signal to come off in its own time.

The natural light and backdrop of the garden both add to this photo, and demonstrate that out in the garden the eye really does focus on the bits it chooses, painting out the rest. Sometimes it is the job of the garden railway builder to create something bland rather than something precise - something that the eye just won't pick up on, such as that rough concrete wall - and this freedom from a constant need for detail, particularly after years of ultra-precise modelling inside, makes garden railway building seem almost a completely different pastime to constructing a line indoors.

ERN
760

My bet is that this otherwise-immaculate Class 50 has been reported with a suspect traction motor, and that the works have sent it out on an empty ballast hopper working to see if the problem is something serious or if it is just a figment of a bored driver's imagination. You can just imagine being stood at the lineside watching this train hammering past, which is one of the real advantages of garden railways in my opinion - the ability to really see trains run for long distances at decent speeds. The tunnel mouth in the background of this view is built up out of small pieces of slate split off a very large block purchased from the garden centre as rockery stone, held together with dabs of mortar as mentioned on page 43.

A Beattie Well Tank drifts gently around Dennis Tillman's garden railway with the afternoon parcels train, heading back up to Exeter perhaps from some far-flung corner of the LSWR's network of lines in the West. The point motors for the junction just in front of the train are the old H and M type, and they have been surviving outside for at least a decade, maintained simply by a once-yearly dose of oil. The centre-over springs probably rusted away years ago, but in 'O' gauge there is more than sufficient resistance from all the slide chairs to hold the switches against the stock rails and prevent trains from derailing in the facing direction.
It seems amazing to think that a sister of the same long-lived class of engines could equally accurately have been painted in BR black and sent round the garden with a rake of china clay hoods to evoke memories of the Wenford Bridge branch in the late 1950s.

What must be quite a short china clay train, judging by the fact the track circuit behind the train has already been cleared and has released the down advance starter, heads across the viaduct into Grogley Junction. This viaduct was built across the edge of the patio for an 'O' gauge garden railway with which I dabbled for a while and it has been pressed into service again for my current garden line. It was originally cast using 10mm aggregate in a mould constructed along the same lines as that shown diagrammatically on the rear cover and the radius of the arches is curiously similar to that of the guttering left over from our extension. The piers are actually separate units, built up out of the same mortar as that used for building construction, and the resulting viaduct is strong enough to easily support my weight.